MISS OLMSTED'S NURSING ADVENTURES

PAMELA LEE

Tigerlily Farm Productions, LLC

Front cover image Gilman Hall, Johns Hopkins University, provided by Karlene Shippelhoute.

DEDICATION

This book is dedicated to my long-time friend, Dr. Michael A. Chapin, Ph.D. Mike assisted with research at Johns Hopkins University, locating Katherine Olmsted's medal collection and Johns Hopkins' nursing school description from the early 1900's. Mike's lovely wife, Karlene Shippelhoute, photographed Gilman Hall at Johns Hopkins University campus for the front cover of this book. Gilman Hall, built in 1876, is the original academic building on the Homewood Campus, which housed the schools of nursing and medicine. Katherine Olmsted's story is complete due to Mike and Karlene's kind assistance. Thank you so much!

Acknowledgements

Thank you to my husband, Richard Lee, for his unending support and patience while the prequel was created. He stepped in to help out where ever needed at the drop of a hat. You are my best friend! Also thank you to Sandi Hamilton, President Town of Sodus Historical Society who cheerfully met us many times for research.

Contents

MISS OLMSTED'S NURSING ADVENTURES

Promise of a Talented Young Woman

Katherine Olmsted had an amazing adventure in Europe while serving as a Red Cross nurse during World War I and later a second tour of duty during post war recovery. She made quite an impact on local communities in war stricken Romania, and provided important reconstruction efforts in post WWI in Europe. Katherine's experience included escaping a siege by the Germans, which was documented in her own words via letters home to her mother, published by the local newspaper in 1918. Katherine worked both in public nursing and Red Cross nursing service for periods throughout her career. Her Red Cross service file is a mixed bag, filled with letters and notes which described her butting heads with Red Cross executives in Washington, D.C. On the other hand, the Red Cross service file also contains numerous job offers over the years.

Katherine started out with humble beginnings and her early years were compiled by the Wallington Schoolhouse Restoration Committee. The Committee did an excellent job in preserving the history of Katherine's younger days and also providing stories from local residents at that time.

"Katherine Olmsted was raised in De Moines, Iowa. She was born in February 1888 and had an older brother, Harry. Her father, Augustus Olmsted managed a branch of the Olmsted Saddlery Company in De Moines. Her mother, Emma Lent Olmsted, was daughter of a successful fruit grower in Wallington, New York, Charles Lent. Katherine, her brother and mother visited her grandparents in Wallington each summer."[1]

Katherine's future career would touch many lives and she became a strong advocate for the public she served. Many people were better off because of her influence, which started with her humble beginnings. "Katherine was a typical teenager who attended High School in De Moines and graduated in 1906, which sadly was the same year her father passed away."[2] "Being a very bright student, she earned a scholarship to the Art Institute of Chicago for one year. After completing one year at art school, Katherine attended the University of Wisconsin for two years to continue her art studies until 1909. Next, she enrolled in the Chicago School of Civic and Philanthropy, but then she changed schools and took a course in social work at Buffalo University."[3] Based on her resume, Katherine studied topics that she may have excelled at or was perhaps interested in, changing direction throughout her college years. It may have been after these first three years that Katherine's aunts, Mary and Kathryn Lent, guided her into nursing. Both aunts were career nurses, as described in the following articles.

According to the local Sodus Newspaper, The Record, Miss Mary Lent was a Chief Nurse of United States Public Health and had graduated from Johns Hopkins Nursing School. Mary Lent was also very prominent in public health nursing in Baltimore, MD and New York and during WWI was chief nurse of the United States Public Health Service.[4]

Kathryn Lent (Katherine's other aunt and namesake) was a surgical nurse for an eye specialist in Iowa and then Arkansas when he moved his practice.[5]

Katherine followed in her Aunt Mary's footsteps and enrolled in the same nursing college, "Johns Hopkins School of Nursing in Baltimore. After completing the three year program, she graduated in 1912 with an R.N. designation."[6]

Johns Hopkins University accepted its first class of students in October 1889 at the School of Nursing. From the beginning, the School demanded high standards of achievement from its nurses in training. Admission requirements were stiff and the course of study evolved into a rigorous three year program of lectures and experience on the hospital wards. The nurses' training school at Hopkins soon gained an international reputation as a leader in nursing training.

The School's first administrators compiled and published texts on principles and methods of nursing, books on the history of nursing and nursing ethics and initiated the first two professional nursing organizations and journals in the United States.[7]

The original academic building on the Homewood campus is Gilman Hall. And still today, Johns Hopkins School of Nursing is regularly ranked among the best graduate schools of nursing in the nation by U.S. News and World Report. [8]

Upon graduation Katherine joined the staff of the Baltimore Visiting Nurse Association, where she worked for a year."[9] A tribute by a fellow Nurse, Alta Dines, provided more information about Katherine's first year of employment.

Katherine worked with her Aunt Mary Lent in the Baltimore Instructive Visiting Association, where she made several outstanding contributions to public health nursing. I remember her as the young public health nurse of the first official Public Health Nursing Film. She had a scintillating personality –great charm – she was a fluent speaker who easily attracted followers wherever she went.[10]

"Katherine's next position was also in Baltimore, Maryland at the Social Service Department of Johns Hopkins University from July 1, 1913 – April 1, 1914 Katherine served as Assistant Director of Social Services and worked in the wards of their hospital."[11] Katherine had returned to the hospital of her Alma Mater for almost a year.

2

Nursing Career Early Days

Not long after Katherine accepted her second job in Baltimore, opportunity came knocking and she moved to a new career in Jacksonville, Illinois. It is quite a distance from Maryland to Illinois, however Jacksonville is only about an hour from the Chicago Art School Katherine attended, and just under a two hour drive from her home in Des Moines, Iowa. "Katherine accepted a position as Executive Secretary at the Western Office of National Public Health Nursing Association in Jacksonville, Illinois. She served in this position for two years from April 1914- February 1916, and as rural public health nurse with the Morgan County, Illinois, Anti-Tuberculosis Association at the same time."[1]

Many Johns Hopkins nurses joined the Red Cross Reserves during World War I, and it may have been possible that enrollment with the Red Cross was encouraged by the university and/or alumnae. Although Katherine was busy serving two jobs, "she applied to the Red Cross reserves in 1914."[2] "Her former training school of nursing provided a recommendation. In November 1914, S.W. Lawler, R.N. of Johns Hopkins Hospital Training wrote a recommendation for Katherine."[3] She continued to work in the nursing field while waiting to be called by the Red Cross, sometimes holding two positions simultaneously.

"Katherine never married and did not have any children of her own."[4] As a single working girl without a young family to care for, Katherine had the time and energy to work two jobs.

The United States Congress voted to go to war in April 1917. Katherine had applied to the Red Cross reserve three years before the United States joined World War I, rather than joining the U.S. Army nursing corps. The stirrings of war in Europe had begun in 1914, but the United States was not a part of the war during the early years. Katherine may have felt a patriotic duty to enlist as a Red Cross reserve nurse in case there ever came a time of great need. She wrote on her annual Red Cross Survey in 1916, "I am ready for duty in case of war in the United States."[5]

"In February 1916 Katherine accepted the position of State Supervising Nurse, Wisconsin Health Department – as health lecturer in charge of Public Health Nursing work in State, and at the same time Director Public Health Nursing course under State T.B. Association, University of Wisconsin. In this second position she pioneered the first Public Health Nursing course."[6] These were both promotions from her past Executive Secretary position. Milwaukee is located about one hour by automobile from Madison, where Katherine's former school, University of Wisconsin, is located. Wisconsin is just north of Illinois. The colleges she attended and positions held in these cities are all within a short driving distance of one another. This cluster excludes Baltimore, Maryland, which is on the Eastern Coast, just south of Pennsylvania.

Before 1920, women in the United States did not have the right to vote and were not recognized as individuals in common law. Typically, women did not have careers outside the home and did not own property. They were expected to keep the home, have children and be occupied with domestic activities. It is important to recognize that Katherine and her aunts were ahead of their time. They were all career ladies, unmarried, owned property and very much entities in their own right. The nursing shortage during the early 1900s may be due to fact that women commonly did not have careers outside the home. These quotes describe Katherine's efforts to raise awareness and recruit nurses,

During her early days in public health nursing, Miss Olmsted wrote articles for both the *American Journal of Nursing* and *Public Health Nursing*. In 1916 she wrote a little pamphlet called *Nursing as a Vocation for Women*, which was published by The University of Wisconsin Extension Division. A statement in this publication has significance for nurses today:

Nurses must be more than trained in certain habits; they must be developed and educated. Although a nurse has completed her prescribed course of study she has not finished her education, just as the true scholar is not finished by school and college. The nurse learns in the training school only the main principals of the science of caring for the sick and the methods of the art of nursing. If she has an open mind and a desire to advance, life outside the school, and years of experience, will add immensely to her knowledge of the science and make her more proficient in the art.

As Director of Public Health Nursing, Wisconsin Anti-Tuberculosis Association, Miss Olmsted developed the public health nursing course and taught it to various groups of nurses. As a teacher, she was especially skillful, and her former students remember her with respect and affection. Miss Olmsted organized and taught the first public health nursing course offered in the state. This was some twenty years before any Wisconsin university offered such a course, and the program had a significant effect on the development of public health nursing in Wisconsin. Nurses serving in newly organized public health departments found they were not prepared for the tasks they faced, and the course provided valuable help at a time when it was desperately needed. This public health course was sponsored by the Wisconsin Anti-Tuberculosis Association and the University Extension Division.[7]

Upon reading of Katherine's accomplishments, it is clear to see how the force of her influence could change a community. The position of Director of Public Health Nursing was a turning point in her career, from student nurse to identifier of needs and teacher in the nursing field. Her ability to observe a situation and create a plan is described in the following newspaper article.

> Miss Katherine Olmsted, R. N., was engaged by the Wisconsin Anti-Tuberculosis Association for the special purpose of developing a recruiting and training plan for state certified public health nurses. Miss Olmsted included many state agencies in the training plan, which provided expertise in many facets, such as; school truancy, legal probation, family relations, poverty, crime, and industry as well as standard hospital training. The course was designed to include practical field work as well, which provided practical experience in various community conditions.
>
> The main objective was to standardize public health nursing service throughout the state. Benefits included increased efficiency of nurses and highest grade of service to the community. By organizing the state nursing program, there was greater recognition both of what the community needed and proper training provided to the nurses.[8]

Katherine had a wide range of experiences while in Wisconsin, such as; writing articles about nursing as a career path for women, developing a public health nurse training course, and teaching the course. There was also an interesting occurrence summarized, as shared by her cousin, Anna W. Olmsted.

> While serving as Supervising Nurse for the Wisconsin Health Department, Katherine had the opportunity to work with American Indians. Katherine directed the construction of a new hospital to take care of the Indian population. She later

learned of an ancient superstition these Indians still practiced. It seemed that whenever a baby was born, the building in which the birth took place had to be burned down because it was thought to be unclean. Well, Katie wasn't about to let the new hospital be burned down, so she incorporated the idea of having tents set up for the Indian squaws in which to give birth to their papooses, and then burn the tents down instead of the hospital.[9]

During this time, Katherine also began to advocate for the public that she served. In a letter to the Superintendent of Nursing Services, Washington, D.C. on December 2, 1916, Katherine wrote,

> "Last week, I managed to persuade two County Boards of Supervisors to make appropriations of $1,500 to hire nurses, automobiles in the spring and expenses of the visiting county nurses. Have not yet been able to find the proper nurses to fill these important positions. On December 4, 1916 the Washington, D.C. Superintendent wrote back, thrilled and had two candidates for Katherine to consider. She also mailed some Red Cross bulletins to Katherine to distribute."[10]

After this positive interaction with the Red Cross and the fact that Katherine was listed as available in the Red Cross Reserves, "she was approached with a job offer and decided to accept a position with Federal Children's Bureau in Washington, DC starting September 1, 1917. However, greater plans were afoot and in July 1917, Miss Clara Noyes at Red Cross Nursing Service offered Katherine the opportunity to go with a special commission to Romania as a Red Cross Nurse."[11] Congress had declared war in April 1917 and America's time of great need had arrived. The American Red Cross had begun sending doctor and nurse units overseas to help in World War I. Katherine's Red Cross assignment arrived and she was very excited. In a letter to Miss Noyes she wrote, "I am more than delighted to go with this commission and think the outdoor uniform and coat are mighty good looking."[12] This is followed by a "telegram from Katherine to Miss Clara Noyes at Red Cross Head Quarters on July 13, 1917. Very anxious to go with special commission to Roumania. How long would I be gone? Please ask Federal Bureau to wait for my return."[13] No correspondence was located in her service file regarding a discussion of pay rate for the Red Cross Nurse position or if Katherine was even aware of the the pay rate at this point. Her career so far in public health nursing did not include combat training for war zone experience and she may not have been prepared for the hardships that she would soon face. "And as for holding her new position at the Federal Children's Bureau, that didn't happen. World War I happened instead."[14]

There was a whirlwind of activity to "get a passport, inoculations up to date, and uniforms issued in time to travel. There are many telegrams and letters in Katherine's Red Cross Service file regarding the preparations. Naturally, all stateside work was quickly released to support the war effort. Katherine was on her way to Romania and was about to have the adventure of a lifetime."[15]

What was particularly important about Katherine's Alma Mater was the support by fellow Johns Hopkins graduate nurses. The nurses formed a network of referrals for nursing positions within the Red Cross which became prominent in World War I.

> The Johns Hopkins Hospital Training School for Nurses, its alumnae, and the nursing profession were all involved in World War I. Johns Hopkins nurses answered the call to serve well before the United States entered the war in 1917, and several alumnae remained in Europe to aid in post war reconstruction. The Great War provided Hopkins nurses with new opportunities to display their leadership in the profession. The war had both a profound effect on individual nurses and raised the profile of the American Red Cross and the nursing profession.

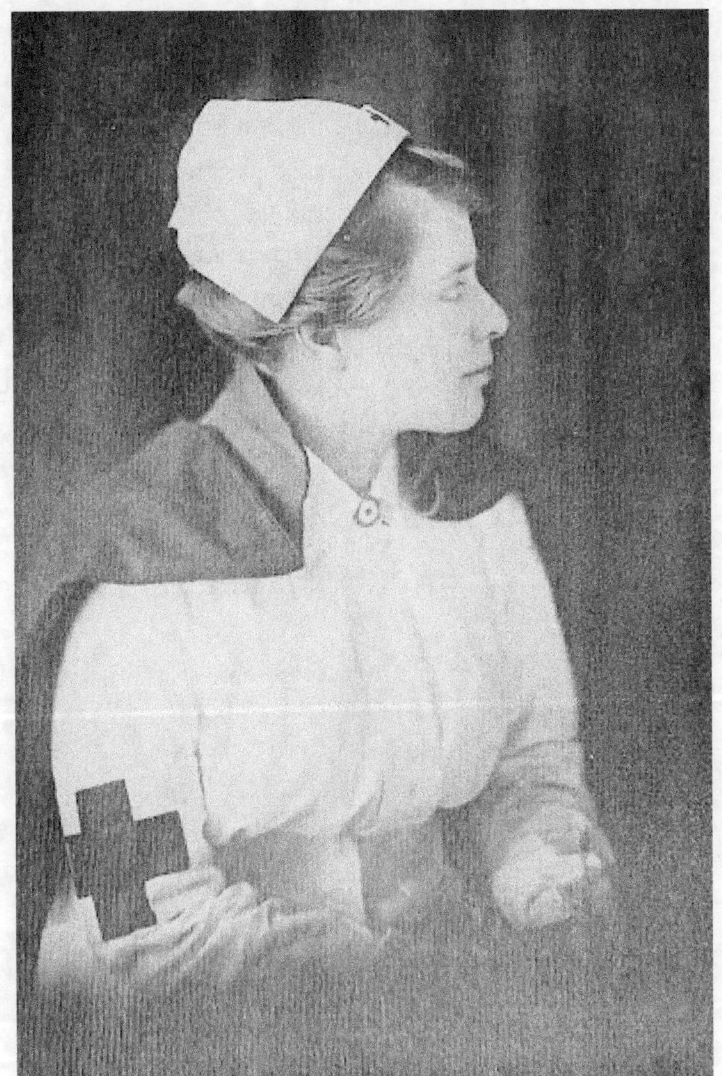

Katherine Olmsted 1917
Sodus Historical Society

The Hopkins nurses who served before US entry into the war were joined by over 200 other alumnae once the US entered the war. After the war, these adventurous women were engaged in efforts to spread the American model of nursing internationally. Hopkins nurses included Florence Patterson (class of 1907), Katherine Olmsted (class of 1912), Alice Fitz-gerald (class of 1906) and Clara Noyes (class of 1896).

By the end of the war, the American Red Cross saw an opportunity to use their nurses' experiences and connections to spread the American model of nursing training to Europe to address the public health needs during European post war reconstruction. While Hopkins alumna Clara Noyes (class of 1896) led the American Red Cross from Washington, D.C., Alice Fitzgerald and Katherine Olmsted led the Nursing Bureau of the newly formed League of Red Cross Societies in Geneva, Switzerland.[16]

3

World War I

So much has been analyzed and written on The Great War, or World War I, that there is a vast amount of information both on-line and at local libraries. An incredibly brief summary of who, where, what and when includes the following.

World War I began in southeastern Europe, in an area referred to as the Balkans, on July 28, 1914. The war involved two rival sets of powers; the German Empire and Austria-Hungary against the Allies, which included Russia, France, the British Empire and later the United States. There were many factors that came into play as to the cause of World War I, such as; political, territorial, fragmented governing, the arms race and economic competition. There was also a complex web of alliances and imperialism. World War I was one of the deadliest global conflicts in history and left millions of military and civilians dead.[1]

The countries that comprise the Balkans include "Yugoslavia, Romania, Bulgaria, Greece and Albania" according to Reader's Digest, 76. "The Red Cross was able to call into the field and send actual help to Allies in Europe. Six base hospital units were sent inside of three weeks over water, where they took over existing hospitals and relieved struggling staffs who were caring for the wounded for the previous three years."[2]

The Red Cross played an important part in World War I and a comprehensive summary is provided by Henry P. Davison, Chairman of the War Council of the American Red Cross.

> On the 10th of May, 1917, President Wilson appointed a War Council for the American National Red Cross and Henry P. Davison was asked to take the chairmanship. The mission was to look after the men of our own Army and to assist the War Department. Nobody could fail to discern the need of Europe, where the war was raging. Thousands of men, women and children were homeless, starving, fleeing before a relentless enemy. Food, clothing and medicine were lacking and disease was raising its ugly head in the wake of death and desolation. The plan divided itself into two problems; first, to get the necessary relief to Europe in the shortest possible time, second, to organize ample means of caring for all the various needs of our own army.[3]

Romania is spelled three different ways in various reports over the years. Romania as written today, Roumania as written in 1917 and Rumania used in 1920 by Davison. The different spellings started to get a little crazy, but it is kept as presented for authenticity sake. The following news article described the specific Red Cross mission which Katherine joined. She may not have realized it, but she was headed into the center of the war.

> ANDERSON TO HEAD RED CROSS UNIT -
> Third American Relief Commission to be Located in Roumania
> As a further step to its program, for basing American relief work abroad on accurate surveys of conditions, the Red

Cross War Council announced the dispatch of "A Red Cross Commission to, Roumania." This is the-third Red Cross" commission, to be sent to Europe since the organization of the War Council. One commission, headed by Major Grayson M. P. Murphy, is already at work In France; a second, under the leadership of Pr. Frank Billings, will arrive in a few days in Russia. The commission to Roumania, which is headed by Henry W. Anderson, a prominent lawyer of Richmond, VA, will undertake an investigation of sanitary and health conditions and provide actual relief work among the Roumanian refugees. To do this work, a Red Cross medical unit of 12 doctors and 12 nurses will accompany the commission. Quantities of medical supplies, serums, vaccines and foodstuffs, urgently needed in Roumania, will be sent with the commission by the War Council.

A special emergency appropriation of 1,200,000 has been voted for Roumanian relief. In addition to Mr. Anderson, the chairman, the members of the commission to Roumania, as announced by Mr. Davison are: Arthur Graham Glasgow, an engineer of Washington, D. C., one of top of the leaders of his profession, who has lived for more than 12 years in London. Dr. Francis W. Peabody of Boston, representing the Rockefeller foundation in its medical Investigations in China. Bernard Flexner of Chicago, a lawyer who has taken a prominent part in many sociological movements In the Middle West. Dr. H. Gideon Wells of Chicago, professor of pathology, University of Chicago. Dr. Roger Griswell Perkins of Cleveland, professor of hygiene, Western Reserve University. Dr. Robert C. Bryan of Richmond, VA is one of the leading surgeons of the south.

Doctors and nurses of the medical unit accompanying the commission are:

Dr. W. D. Kirkpatrlck, Bellingham, Wash.

Dr. Richard Penn Smith, Fort Loudon, Pa.

Dr. D.J. McCarthy, Davenport, Iowa

Dr. George Y. Massenburg. Macon, Ga.

Dr. R H. Rulison,
Dr. B. C. Hamilton, Syracuse, N. Y.
Dr. Benjamin Earl LeMaster, Macomb, IU.V
Dr. Louis H. Llmauvo, Lynn, Mass.
Dr.-E. F. Hlrd, Bound Brjooft,
Dr. W. T. Lowe, Pine Bluff, Ark.
Dr. Joseph P. H. Gruener
Dr. George Duro Guca, Chicago
Dr. William J. Kucera, New Prague, Minn.
Florence Patterson, head nurse, Washington. D. C.
Rachel C. Torrance, New York
Katherine Olmsted, Milwaukee, Wis.
Alma Forester, Chicago
Alice Gilborne, Chicago
Anna T. Pederson, New York.[4]

The article stated, a unit of 12 doctors and 12 nurses accompanied the commission, however, the unit roster at the end of the same article included the names of 13 doctors and 6 nurses. It may have been easier to find male/doctors willing to enlist overseas and more difficult to find female/nurses. "Katherine's service file contains her considerable documented efforts to raise awareness of the need of nurses, and she even wrote an article titled "Dearth of Nurses".[5]

The Red Cross planned to provide medical supplies with the deported unit. Along with the nurses and doctors listed, the news article also listed six gentlemen accompanying the Red Cross Unit including an engineer, lawyer, two professors, a surgeon and a representative from the Rockefeller Foundation. The war effort garnered a lot of support to aid relief.

4

❧

The Journey 1917

An outline of the Red Cross Unit's itinerary is located in the National Archives. "The American Red Cross Mission to Romania unit did not travel the shortest distance to Romania. Instead, they took the long route westward"[1], which is easily twice the distance to Romania than if the unit had sailed out of New York City to England and then Europe.

It appeared that no change was made in the travel send-off in spite of the ensuing war. According to the itinerary, "they departed from Chicago at 6:30 p.m. on July 28, 1917 via the Soo Line and Canadian Pacific railway. The unit traveled westward across North America to reach Vancouver, British Columbia on North America's west coast on Wednesday, August 1st, 1917. This travel segment across land lasted four days."[2] "The reason for the circuitous route over the Pacific was to avoid submarine warfare in the Atlantic."[3]

AMERICAN RED CROSS MISSION TO ROUMANIA.

Suggested Itinerary.

Saturday July 28 - Leave Chicago 6:35 PM via Soo Line and
Canadian Pacific Railway.

Sunday   "   29 - Enroute via St Paul.

Monday   "   30 -   "

Tuesday   "   31 -   "

Wednesday Aug. 1 - Due to arrive Vancouver 9:25 AM (Hotel Vancouver)

Thursday   "   2 - Sail at 11 AM by Canadian Pacific R. M. S.
Empress of Russia calls at Victoria about 5:00PM.

Monday   " 13 - Due to arrive Yokohama. Leave Yokohama 9:51 PM by
rail for Tsuruga.

Tuesday   " 14 - Due to arrive Tsuruga 10:40 AM. Leave Tsuruga 5:00 PM
by Russian Volunteer Fleet Steamer.

Wednesday   " 15 - Enroute.

Thursday   " 16 - Due to arrive Vladivostock 9:00AM. Leave Vladivostock
10:00 PM by Courier Train via Trans-Siberian Railway.

Saturday   " 25 - Due to arrive Petrograd 9:55 PM.

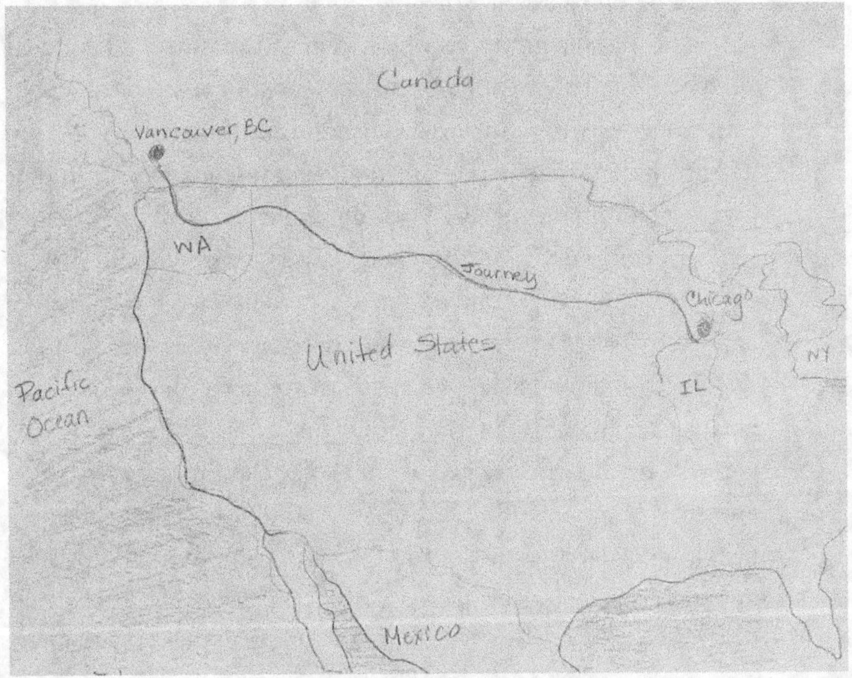

Journey from Chicago, IL to Vancouver, BC
Sketch by Pamela lee

"Upon reaching Vancouver, the unit sailed the next day on Thursday, August 2, 1917 on the Empress of Russia from Vancouver, BC to Yokahama, Japan, across the Pacific Ocean."[4]

Katherine wrote from the ship: Russia is so upset that it is just a big question what we will have when we get there, and what we can do if we do get there. We will be terribly disappointed if we cannot make our study of Roumania, as the outline for the plan of work is so very interesting. The American Minister to Roumania who is on board tells us that the Roumanian Government and the Queen are eager to welcome us and are preparing a chateau to house us. A Roumanian doctor is giving us lessons in the Roumanian language and we are besides cramming on Russian.

I like the group very, very much. The nurses all seem to be specialists in some line or other – most of them have served in Europe before-in Bulgaria, Germany and Russia. The doctors are great-they take good care that we are comfortable and it gives us confidence. We are taking eight carloads of supplies with us; equipment for a 100 bed hospital has been shipped by the Red Cross to Roumania-but we may never see it. The unit arrived in Yokohama, Japan twelve days later.

In a later letter: We spent a wonderful week in Japan and we are wild about that beautiful, artistic country where we were royally entertained at the American Embassy in Tokyo and by the Japanese Red Cross. We had a fascinating time at a big dinner given for us by the Red Cross; ate with chopsticks out of the prettiest lacquered dishes and even tasted the raw fish and raw birds-we had tea every time we turned around. Also we have received such lovely presents-fans, flowers, fruit and we went to their unique theatre and rode in picturesque jinrickshas.

The Red Cross group took a train to Tauruga, Japan where they were to meet a Russian Volunteer Fleet Steamer ship. "After a ride on a queer jerky little Japanese train and a very rough passage over the Japan sea, we arrived at Manchuria in Vladivostock, a horribly dirty city, half Chinese, half Russian, crowded with beggars and soldiers.[5]

According to the itinerary, "crossing Japan by train then the Japan Sea by ship took approximately three days. The unit should have arrived in Vladvistock on Thursday, July 16th at 9:00 a.m. and left at 10:00 a.m. that same morning by Courier Train via the Trans-Siberian Railway to arrive in Petrograd on July 25, 1917. However, on the ground war conditions caused the unit to arrive later than the scheduled."[6]

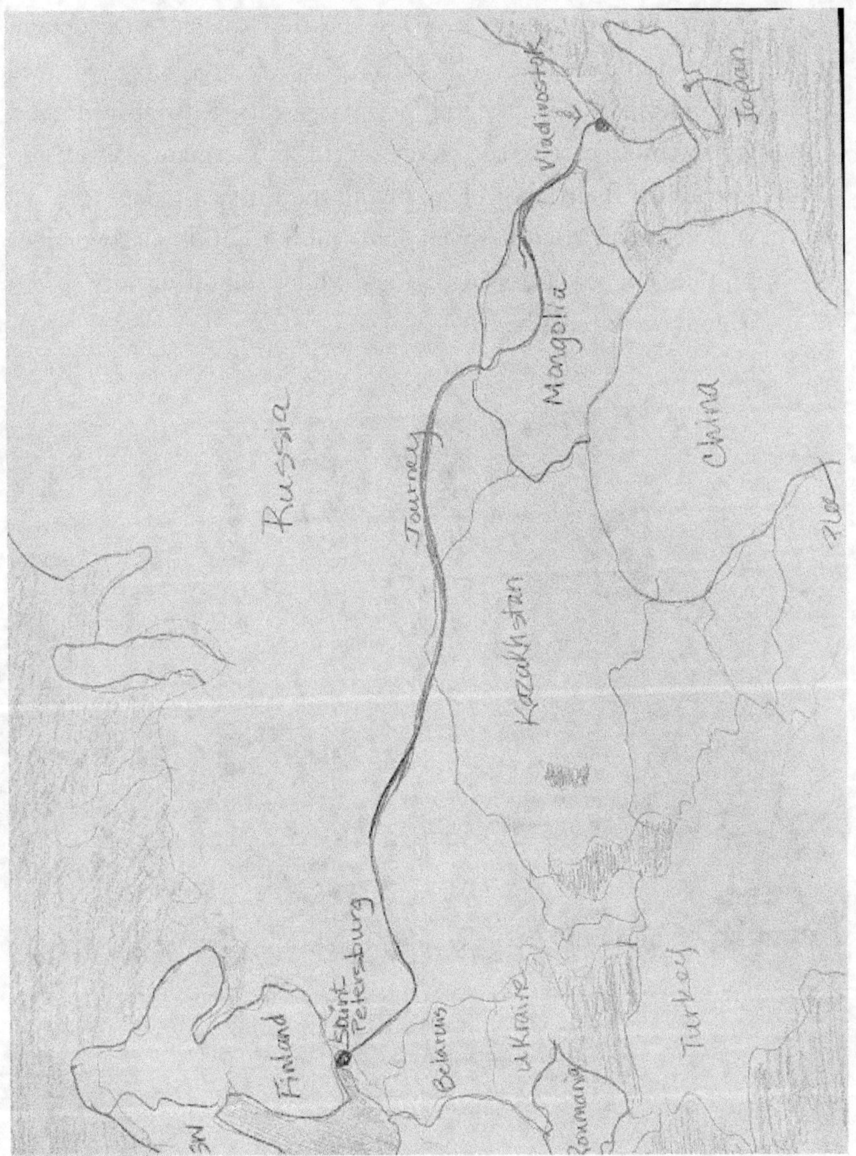

Map from Vladivostok to Saint Petersburg
Sketch by Pamela Lee

Davison, Chairman of the War Council of ARC, kept tabs on each Red Cross mission that was sent to Europe. "To reach Rumania, the Red Cross Mission was compelled to journey by Vladivostok and cross the long reaches of Siberia.

It was met with every courtesy by the Russian government, but underneath the visible surface Russia was honey-combed with German intrigue and German agents. Russian railroads, for the most part in the secret control of Germany, lagged and miscarried their labor of supplying the Russian troops. On the wharves of Vladivostok were lying millions of dollars' worth of supplies for the Russian soldiery which should have been delivered three years before."[7]

Russian woman serving as an Assistant Fireman on the Trans-Siberia Railway
National Geographic Magazine, Sep 1916

On account of war conditions, with no trains running normally, the United States Ambassador to Japan had arranged with Kerensky to send a special train for the safe conduct of the Americans. Warned about the scarcity of food in Russia, the unit was well supplied with canteens and hard tack.

The train was waiting for them when they arrived in Vladivostock and proved to be the imperial train of Czar

Nicholas II returning from depositing the Czar and his ill-fated family at Tobolsk. And what a train! There were nine cars with women firemen and women engineers, a freight car full of supplies, a baggage car, and a car at the rear containing livestock, animals and birds of various sorts used for food. Katherine wrote; It was the most enormous train I had ever seen. You had to get up into it on a tall ladder.[8]

Military members of the American Mission to Russia in the apartments of the former Tsar on the Imperial Train in which they traveled from Vladivostok to Petrograd
National Geographic Magazine, August 1917

In the quarters reserved for the Royal family sleeping cars were provided with a row of staterooms. The double bedsteads were of gold plate, which was also on the red velvet upholstered furniture: heavy linen sheets had large embroidered crests: tapestries hung on the walls: bookcases were filled with hand bound books; thick red velvet carpets covered the floor. There were a dining car, crew quarters and even a swimming pool built like a Roman bath with steamer chairs surrounding it. This pool was hailed with delight until it was discovered that the crew bathed in it and that the water had not been changed since the beginning of the Revolution!

From Katherine's description: A deep toned dinner bell with chimes summoned us to meals-four sumptuous meals served every day; breakfast with porridge and sweet things like pastry or cake; one o'clock brought a luncheon with several courses-one plate put on top of another at each place until the soup plates rested under our chins; at four o'clock a high tea-like a larger than ordinary dinner; at nine o'clock came the heaviest repast of the day-dinner with six or seven courses-with fish, fowl, pelican (like skinny chicken)-four or five dark red meats-wild boar, venison, bear-plus six kinds of dessert-and special wines accompanied each course. A far cry, this, from the canteens and hardtack which had been provided!

The trip consumed nearly five weeks-although an American train could have made it in five or six days-the journey made endlessly long because of stops at innumerable stations-sometimes to secure new crews, usually to cut wood-often to enable the crew to go fishing. The National Archives itinerary indicates this leg of the journey should have taken about nine days.

At many of the towns some sight-seeing was enjoyed-in Irkutsk, in Ekaterinburg, a little village in the Ural Mountains and especially in Moscow, and there was rejoicing over the occasional appearance of large samovars of boiling water for baths or to wash clothes.

As the train proceeded across the long reaches of Siberia, at stop after stop political exiles who had heard of a Revolution in Russia and had walked hundreds of versts to the railroad climbed aboard. They hung on to car tops and steps, crowded into the cars and the swimming pool, which was emptied to accommodate them. The doctors doubled up in the gold plated bedsteads to make room for elderly refugees and such political exiles as professors and university students-some of whom spoke nine or ten languages. They were fed by the crew and supplies began to run short.[9]

A verst is "a Russian measure of distance equivalent to 3,500 feet or 0.6629 mile."[10] The political exiles, desperate in an attempt to leave the area, walked for long durations in search of trains or other means to depart the country.

Before the journey ended, Katherine mischievously persuaded one of the doctors to pry off the iron coat-of-arms with the double headed eagle from the Czar's coach, a feat accomplished in the darkness of night. This heavy relic was carried in her duffle bag until it was finally brought back to America. Of course if found she might have been liquidated on the spot. The loss was never discovered, however, for the day after the arrival in Petrograd the Czar's train was bombed off the face of the earth by the Bolsheviks![11]

Iron Coat of Arms from Czar Nicholas II's Imperial Train
The Story of an American Red Cross Nurse, Anna W. Olmsted

The Journey did indeed take longer than the itinerary estimated. The first leg across the United States to Vancouver, British Columbia was right on point at about four days, the ocean voyage to Japan was about 12 days and the itinerary estimated 10 days. However, the itinerary didn't count a week spent in Japan and had the unit moving out the next day from Yokohama to Tsuruga. From Tsuruga to Vladivostok appears to be a three day travel, just as the itinerary outlined. However, the train substitution from Vladivostok to Petrograd took much longer. Here the itinerary estimated nine days, and as Katherine indicated, this leg of the journey took nearly five weeks.

Davison shared a perception on the transport situation in his book. "The Red Cross Mission was ushered with all politeness and greatest possible expedition into Rumania but thereafter could secure almost no transport for the material of relief. Russia played them false and was even now on the brink of a German peace."[12]

5

Romania

**Alexander Kerensky (in automobile) as
Minister of War, reviewing Russian troops at
the front**
National Geographic Magazine, July 1917

It appeared that the Czar's train took the Unit directly to Romania rather than Petrograd, as indicated in the itinerary. The distance between Romania and Petrograd is about a half hour by car, very close. "Kerensky met the doctors and nurses at the train station in Romania and gave them bags of money with his portrait included. He decorated each one of them with small Russian medals, along with some supplies."[1]

Russian Freedom Medal
presented to Katherine Olmsted by Russian Premier Alexander
Kerensky

**Johns Hopkins
University, Sheridan
Libraries and Museums**

The medal is a circular, copper colored with the portrait
and inscribed name of A. F. Kerenski, Russian Premier 1917 on
front, cannon and inscription "Za svobodu Rossii vpered"!" (For
the freedom of Russia forward!) on back. Attached to a blue
ribbon with two vertical white stripes with thin black stripes
on either side of the white stripes.[2]

"Queen Marie of Roumania sent a train to bring the Red Cross Unit
to Jassy, which was the new seat of the Roumanian Government after
the Germans took Bucharest. The hospitals were now controlled by
the Germans and only five doctors remained in the city. The promised
chateau was no longer available and the unit was billeted in homes."[4]
"Billet means lodging for a soldier, student, etc., as in a private home or
nonmilitary public building."[5]

Russian Cross
gifted to Katherine Olmsted from Count Alexis Romanoff

**Johns Hopkins
University, Sheridan
Libraries and Museum**

At this same point, the unit also received Russian crosses from Count Alexis Romanoff, of the Russian nobility. It is a silver cross with some green and blue enamel on the front, attached to a small chain of four silver metal links.[3]

Katherine wrote to her family in Wallington, and her letters were later published by the local newspaper. The story of her adventure in Europe is best heard through her own words. Katherine wrote; "We will have been here three weeks tomorrow" on October 4, 1917 which indicated an arrival date of September 14, 1917. Doing some quick math, and knowing the departure date was July 28, 1917, it is estimated that their journey took approximately seven weeks in total. And after this lengthy journey, the unit does not see any war action until October 9, 1917, approximately three weeks after their arrival according to the letters.

Jassy, Roumania
American Red Cross Mission,
% American Legation,
October 4th, 1917

Just heard that they were sending a pouch from the legation today, so will send a note tor you and you stand a little better chance of getting it. You are all having the luck, we are getting very little mail. Some of the nurses have not heard a word since coming. A few letters have come through. I received a note from Mother and was tickled to get a word.

One seems a long way off and all is so tense here. It would be a relief at times if something would explode right in front of us. The air is so full of suppressed excitement and every night I wake up and hear tramp, tramp, tramp, under the window, or horses, heavy wagons or maybe ambulances coming in covered with dust and filled so full.

We are billeted out in different houses by the police. Poor people, they must each take so many soldiers. Many of them have fled and left all their belongings. The Roumanians are fighting very well and we like them so much but if the line gives way at the north in Russia, we are surrounded.

We leave tonight for Roman. A sort of freight car on a military train arrives at 4 a.m. We expect a pleasant but none too comfortable trip. Pleasant because we go to our hospital in Roman quite near the front and we are anxious to get to work. We have been here three weeks tomorrow, loafing and eating food that the starving people need, and doing nothing. We are eager to get to our work at a surgical hospital with about 500 beds, started by the British who are leaving, tired out. Only two doctors and only four nurses left. A miserable hole but we have scoured the country and it is located in the best place. We will clean it up and if we can only get supplies we will be all right now. We brought some with us but only a drop in the bucket. We fear our equipment sent by Archangel is sunk, as we cannot find it. We have sent for more and will trust to luck and Russia to get them to us. Both seem equally uncertain now. A hospital seems as good a place of work as we can man until we get more supplies.

Public health is nil here. No relief agencies. Nothing to give that they need so badly. The town of 290,000 population now harboring 400,000 is not willing to think of sanitation or anything but bread so it is with the entire place. Later we are planning to do extensive work out from our hospitals. As soon as things come we think we will take over a hospital in Jassy for fever cases. All the women have of course been turned out of the hospitals and infant mortality is appalling. We will try to help women and children. Our Colonel has, I believe, already promised to care for 1,600 children, poor, pale, starved little orphans. I hope that I have charge of that work, at a large country place in all probability. The dearest things, such huge, dark eyes and poor, thin little faces! We have visited many hospitals here and they have no nurses, just volunteers who go in without training a few hours a day. There is a shortage of everything. In one hospital 600 pints of milk are allowed and they can get but two quarts a day. Other things in the same proportion. Gauze, cotton and drugs are not to be had, but with all the hardships, the hospitals look remarkably clean here and in some ways are marvelous.

The front is in the mountains here, impossible for ambulances to get near the wounded. Must be carried by men for six miles, so they reach us in bad shape, as there are few men to carry them.

You would laugh if you could see us with our bundles, prepared for a hasty tramp across country. A large colored Jap handkerchief with malted milk tablets, a can of coffee, a bit of tea and hardtack. We have been having hardtack and clear coffee for breakfast in our rooms as a rare treat. We brought the coffee with us. They don't eat breakfast here; just have tea and it don't just taste right in the morning. We eat at the officers headquarters. I have a General on one side who speaks only French and on the other one who speaks only German and two words of English, "Good bye". He is most tall and dignified and when we were introduced on coming into the dining room the first night he said he spoke English, so with a great bow and much flourish, he said, "Good bye". We nearly died laughing.

We have been taking French lessons mornings as everyone here speaks that language.

If we can show the natives how to care for their sick, we will have done much. Of course, eleven nurses with two hospitals of 500 each seems a lot, but it is better than they have and we will teach them. If things clear up we hope to get more American nurses. Typhus is starting now. We visited several hospitals here and it would make your heart ache to see the care, the needless suffering – all, all so different from America. We could scarcely believe it. I have been well but have lost twenty pounds as we have seen no butter, meat, milk or eggs. However I am feeling fine and getting quite toughened. [6]

"Epidemic typhus generally occurs in outbreaks when poor sanitary conditions and crowding is present. It is spread by body lice. Common symptoms include fever, headache, and a rash. Treatment is with the antibiotic doxycycline and reduced exposure to lice will prevent typhus."[7] According to Davison on page 244, "the relief work in Jassy and many of the outlying districts was well organized though hampered by the fatal lack of supplies. The hospitals at Roman and in Jassy with their 500 beds were doing a distinguished work with the limited facilities available."

Roman, October 9, 1917

We traveled to Roman two days ago to take over a British hospital or rather a hospital taken over by them a year ago. They only signed up for a year and it has been a pretty tough pull. They all want to go home. There are only two doctors and six nurses for a six hundred bed hospital. They are busy all the time and expecting to run any minute. They are all eager to get away and I cannot blame them much. We are traveling to run the hospital and a big operating room without gauze, cotton, rubber goods or any medicine. It is going to be interesting to see how it can be done. Have not heard a word from our supplies. Feel sure now they must have been sunk.

They had a hard time here last winter to obtain food and it is pretty cold, but we are prepared for everything, so will not mind it much. Our new hospital is large and imposing from the outside. We go under a tower effect for a gate, under which stands day and night a guard, armed with a long gun and bayonet and a bright red coat, white trousers and blue leggings. He never stops anyone and I really don't see his official value, but it may show up later.[8]

Ancient Gateway Tower, Transylvania,
Hungary 1916
National Geographic Magazine, Feb 1917, Erdelyl

When you enter the hospital, you see long rows of beds, homemade cot affairs. Most of our patients are right sick, all bed cases, because not far from here is a convalescent camp.

They are wretched, poor sick souls. Many are dying. Some are moaning, others praying, some are singing, but all are as brave as brave can be. No complaining. Twice a day they have a hunk of black bread and a dish of sour cabbage soup or a few beans and the rest of the time pain. In the morning they are all brought on stretchers to the operating room and dressed. While away the ward orderly shakes up straw on their cots and perhaps puts a clean, sheet on the bed. They never have more than one.

I am in charge of the dressing room and such a place. They have eight dressings being done at once. Such cries and moans! One fainted this morning and we had no spirits of ammonia. We hadn't a hypodermic and we haven't morphia or didn't have then. Now some of our supplies, mostly private ones of the doctors, have all been put into active use. How long they will last we know not.

The British have worked hard for months. Their only operating table was three big wooden boxes placed together, but lately they secured a table. Much is still missing that usually belongs to a hospital.

Women are rounded up by the police each morning to do the laundry work out of doors. Tubs are hewn out of logs. No boards, wringers or anything; scarcely any soap. They just rinse, beat, rinse, beat - all day. They are given so many sheets or gowns and must turn just so many in at night or no pay.[9]

Women carrying water from wells in Roumania
National Geographic Magazine, Sep 1916 E.M. Newman

These people are like children in many ways; take everything they want. We lock up the cake of soap in the operating room the minute the doctor is through with it or no soap. Everything is under lock and key. I have never seen anything to equal it. The English nurses will not even leave their clothes out on a chair while they sleep.

These simple folk are indeed simple with no idea of sanitation or modesty but with all their faults these peasants are fascinating with dark long hair, rosy cheeks and black eyes. The men wear white homespun blouses, bright sashes and fur vests. The women wear brilliant costumes and all barefooted. The up patients parade the wards in bare legs and feet and short white night skirts to the knees and a bright red flannel jacket. The English brought red jackets and our patients have them. Some have but one leg, one arm, one eye, and such horrible sights.

Our hopes are now that some of us will go to the typhus

hospital in Jassy, others to do more public health work and care for many children. Needless to say I want the last and will probably get it shortly. We think it best to start one thing at a time. Public health work is needed so much here. The wounded are taken care of in a way, but the mothers and children are dying, and babies are no more. It is sad to see their pale little faces and the hungry look in the women's eyes. We are billeted some distance from the hospital and it will be a dark walk in the cold mornings and another at night but we would rather live away. It gives us a change.[10]

Davison was entirely aware of the desperate situation overseas. "When it came to Jassy, the Mission brought with it only the smallest of supplies. In that land of desolation and want they vanished in a day. It was not a question of studying the need of Rumania, the need of Rumania was a nightmare."[11]

October 10, 1917

Well, today things went off much better. The dressing room was a howling, smelly place all day, but I reached home to-night at ten o'clock, feeling quite a deal more cheerful. Today three orderlies made dressings all day, so things are ready for morning. All our patients must be dressed daily, as they are all horribly infected cases. All is quite still now and may remain so, but shortly after the cold comes, the typhus will begin. Last year whole towns were completely wiped out so we are preparing for a busy time soon. We are cleaning patients, whitewashing walls and working like mad to get our hospital spick and span. Tonight our first outpatient or sorted work began. We heard of a sick baby so our head physician and Miss Rowland, a Hopkins Nurse, and a dear went out to see it and brought the child into the hospital. There is great excitement. The soldiers are too delighted and too funny for words. The nurses took two hours for making the baby comfortable in a straw mattress and then locating the mattress where the night nurse could watch it. We have a very good child specialist with us and all things point to some good work along the line.

Things are uncertain yet but our Colonel has promised the Queen to care for 1,000 children and he is of firm belief that the civilian population and public health is our biggest work here. Dr. Perkins, a really very capable man from Western Reserve University, is making plans to clear Roumania of typhus fever by December 1st, so things are moving. We are preparing our hospital to receive typhus cases and also planning a protection for ourselves, which is so complete that we could not possibly get it. The only way to contract the disease is by the bite of the body lice and we have regular suits that they cannot bite through. We will probably bathe every four hours and change all clothing. It seems a terrible nuisance, but the head doctor was in Servia last year and all the nurses took sick. He doesn't intend to let it happen again.

On Sunday mornings only we have clear coffee and it surely is a treat. Other mornings we have a mixture of coffee and wheat ground up. The English nurses willed us a chunk of automobile tire and showed us how they nailed strips of the same on their shoe soles to save their shoes. It is most necessary here. I tell you we have no hot water. All must be brought from our laundry stoves, even for the operating room.

Well, we named the baby Marie after Queen Marie of this country. She is a beautiful and wonderfully enabled woman. Everyone is wild about her. She has been lovely to us and we expect her out soon to see the hospital. She is an Englishwoman and very intelligent and very fond of Roumania. She knows it from A to Z.[12]

Queen Marie of Roumania 1917
Sodus Historical Society

Davison, Chairman of the War Council of the American Red Cross, provided a description of Queen Marie and her active support of her country. She was a very hands on ruler.

There was no sadder and nobler figure than Marie of Rumania, a Queen, who is every inch a woman and who had been trying at the cost of every conceivable sacrifice, with a courage equaled only by her devotion, to stem the tide of suffering.

Utterly fearless, she had gone among her starved and scourge-ridden people like an angel, carrying such food and clothing and medicine as she could gather among those who themselves had nothing. Into a typhus hospital where hundreds lay dying of smallpox, into the horrible dugouts of the refugees, into every place where there was a mouth she could feed or a soul she could cheer, day by day went the Queen of Rumania, and yet, by some strange dispensation, she lived.[13]

Katherine's letter home is continued and describes what she saw and experienced at ground zero.

> Continued - I wish you could see the quaint little mud houses, all scattered anywhere, painted blue or pink with thatched roofs and queer little set in windows. It is a darling little village and very artistic. Geese wander up and down the streets and every family has at least one pig in the little front yard. There is one right under my window now and it squeals occasionally as the goose pinches its leg, although they seem very friendly. This morning as I came out I saw a big rat asleep on top of the nice little pig and I had to step over both to get out of the doorway.
>
> I am living in quite a luxurious house, electric lights, etc., the home of a General who is at the front. We are trying to fix up the hospital, but you cannot buy anything here, not one inch of window glass, nor an inch of pipe to run water through, no nails, not even a pin or needle – things we never think of living without and just what we need the most. As I have said before, would that we could run over to New York for a day or two and buy supplies, but it took us ten weeks to get here and our supplies have not arrived yet. It is useless to try to have things sent. We boil up our instruments, etc. on little alcohol lamps and when that runs out I don't know what we will do. The two English doctors have, since January 1st 1917, up

to the present time performed 1,237 large operations and have been very busy in the dressing room. They are often redressing wounds until twelve o'clock and after a battle constantly for three or four days. We are so busy now and have more nurses and doctors, so we got through about five o'clock to-night. I was about to start cleaning up and felt delighted because I thought I would be through by 8 p.m. dinner time, when they announced two emergency amputations of legs, so I had to give the anesthetic and didn't get away even for dinner. It is nearly midnight now so I must close. We are allowed to send two letters at a time. We know so little about the war or how things are going. We are hidden away down here without a sign or a newspaper or mail. We know only about our bit of front and that is all.[14]

A 1916 National Geographic article, "Roumania and its Rubicon provided a good explanation of the social and political climate in Romania. The Red Cross unit had entered an impoverished country located on the war front. The larger cities were not metropolises of industry and Romania's development was lagging far behind the United States. Most areas were largely rural with rudimentary agricultural roots.

Few states in history have been called to such momentous decisions as Roumania faced when it plunged boldly into the blood and carnage that has rolled over Europe these two long years. This little kingdom is less than one-fifth as big as Texas.[15]

Map of European Countries
Sketch by Pamela Lee

In Europe, the countries are so small and closely located, the populations identify with Bessarabia, Russia and Transylvania, Hungary and Bukowina, Austria. Roumanian people yearn for a restored Roumania under one flag, however joined the Allies in fear of Russia strangulation or causing extinction. If

Russia holds Constantinople, it means strangulation for Roumania. The location of Roumania at the mouth of the Danube causes the country to depend entirely on the Dardanelles. Not only is the cheap waterway an absolute necessity for the bulky products-corn, petroleum and timber—which form the chief exports of Roumania, but these also form the chief exports of Russia, who may rule Roumania completely out of competition. Roumania is made up of a million small farmers and only a few thousand large ones. With so many small farms, naturally a prolific farming population has little money to buy machinery and must be content with the ways and methods of past generations.

Roumania proper is a country of 53,000 square miles and a population of less than eight million. It is slightly larger than Pennsylvania and has half a million fewer people. The country is governed by a king, who is a constitutional monarch and a parliament made up of a Senate and a Chamber of Deputies. Annual income of $1,880 a year is required to become a Senator. Both Senators and Deputies are elected by vote, with voting not weighted equally. 50 general populous votes equal one property owner's vote. Women do not have a right to vote. Military service is compulsory for every boy for two – three years.

There is a vast difference between wealthy large farms and the millions of peasant owned farms. The big estate has every sort of farm machinery compared to similar U.S. farms; mower, steam gang plow, riding cultivator, manure spreader, steam header and thresher. Peasant farms still harvest grain with a sickle, thresh it with the flail or tread it out with oxen and winnow it with the home-made fork.[16]

Roumanian girl coming from market
*National Geographic Magazine, Sep 1916 Frederick
Moore*

Market place in a Roumanian Town
National Geographic Magazine, Feb 1917

The great bulk of Roumania's population belongs to the peasant class. Many of these peasants live on the great estates, where their forbearers for generations have farmed for the absentee landlords. It is regarded as worthy of honor to be the head of a numerous family. The bottle-fed baby is almost unknown in peasant Roumania, which tends to overcome the high infant mortality that would otherwise result. Many of the people are illiterate and there is a high adult death rate, which is common in many lands.

Roumania was one of the most backward nations of Europe forty years ago. There is no tap water in houses in Roumanian villages. Women carrying water from common well pumps is a typical sight. Prince Charles of Prussia was called to throne and set to work immediately to bring the country up to a higher standard. Prince Charles died soon after the European war began. The present king is a nephew of King Carol. His wife (Marie) is a granddaughter of Queen Victoria, and therefore a first cousin of most of the reigning heads of Europe.[17]

Queen Marie described the war situation over the last year to the Red Cross Commissioner with the unit on location. Here is an excerpt from the Red Cross Commissioner's report, in her own words.

Her Majesty reported that the retreat from Wallachia, and the sorrow and depression of a vanquished Army is a story filled with tragic grief; the winter was one of the darkest horror, thousands of our soldiers died of sheer want. We could neither feed, clothe, warm nor house them. Disease at its worst form fell upon us; and being cut off from all aid, we struggled against odds we had no means of overcoming. Row upon row of graves and uncounted numbers of rough wooded crosses throughout the land stand as mute witness of a tale too sad to relate. Thousands of little children, left without father or mother, died before help could reach them, and I, the Queen, heard each cry of anguish, shared each terror, and divided each fear. Then spring came – and as by a miracle, our armies seemed to have a rebirth. The specters that had haunted our streets in winter became soldiers once more. Our thinned ranks were filled up. A new desire for vengeance and intense longing for homes taken away by the enemy steeled every heart for a new effort. But our newborn hopes were destined to wither away. The Russian revolution had sown discord and disorganization in the hearts of our nearest allies, and when the great hour for action came – the hour which our army had hungered for, and into which our troops had thrown themselves with a bravery that justified our dearest hopes – our neighbors failed us.[18]

Roumanians whose ancestors crossed the Transylvania Alps, now residents of Wallachia
National Geographic Magazine, Sep 1916 Erdelyl

Wallachian mountain folk
National Geographic Magazine, Sep 1916 Erdelyl

According to Katherine's letters, the Red Cross Unit had been at the hospital in Roman for less than a week and had relieved the doctors and nurses, who had been stationed there for almost three years. She described the living conditions for the patients as well as the medical staff in the war torn country, in the following letter.

Roman, October 10, 1917

I am afraid I have told all the unpleasant things about our hospital. It is quite true they are most in evidence, but that fact alone makes us glad we came and makes it worthwhile. We have removed casts, and cleaned out hundreds of worms and maggots. We have located pus pockets and stopped fearful agony.

They are so grateful—they are so grateful. They are the bravest things in the world, yet just like children if one gets a pill the whole ward cries for pills. They actually cry too and such jabbering. They have large supplies of some sweet sort of a tonic. They all love it and we almost died the first day to see a Russian sister take a big black bottle and one spoon and give each patient a does all out of the very same spoon, down the long row of beds. Pour souls when we cannot get food to get them two meals a day.

We have some queer languages floating around. We have French patients, some English, lots of Russian, German and Austrian prisoners sick, hundreds of Roumanians, many Serbians, Bohemians, Armenians, Turks, Egyptians, Bulgarians and now Americans. I am learning some unusual languages. We have one word for water in the dining room, another in the ward, another in the dressing room and still another in the operating room, all according to the nationality of your orderly in that place, and you must learn the word or you don't get what you want.

My roommate is a Miss Gilbourne from Chicago, has just announced that I may have six ounces of warm water from the alcohol lamp for a bath, so I must hurry before she drinks it. This is a mighty dry country, and even water is scarce.

October 12, 1917

It is black out tonight. Aeroplanes and other things roam around on black nights in these countries, so searchlights are flashing constantly in the skies. What they would do if they saw anything I don't know. I know what I would do.

We walked down to see the Russian trenches today. They are very interesting and some of the Roumanian officers are to take us all around their front someday soon in a car.

Great excitement today! We are going to have some laundry work done. We have been gone now for twelve weeks and have been able to get laundry done once in that time. We wash our things as we need them ourselves. Fearful nuisance. Laundry is a big problem. Soap is like gold, water is scarce and labor not to be had. I do hope some of us can get out of this hospital soon. We feel such a need for outside work, but as yet we could go little. We are so handicapped by the language, the customs, the absolute lack of law and authority and interest in health conditions at this strenuous time. After the war that work could be done with great success, but now even if they need it more they will not accept it. I am afraid you cannot force it upon them.

We hope to do much cleaning up to prevent typhus. They are deathly afraid of it and it is our hold on them. Poor souls. Don't know yet if the nurses will get out into the homes. Our doctors are so afraid we will catch typhus. I doubt if they will let us. It would be difficult to protect ourselves and we may have to depend upon workers who have had the have had the disease to do that part, and get all the cases in the hospital where they can be properly isolated and parted from the much to be dreaded body lice.

We had a flag raising party to day and farewell to the English and a real party for all the hospital employees. Most of the town inhabitants came along, too. They love festive occasions and surely do dress up from head to heels with cross stitch on wonderful handmade linen, beads and brassy jewelry and all sorts of quaint arrangements on heads and feet.[19]

Typical Roumanian costumes of the Carpathian and Eastern Alps regions
National Geographic Magazine, Sep 1916, Erdelyl

These people never have had outdoor sports so the English doctors taught them some games, race, tug of war, etc. We had a fine time, had a sort of ice cream and some cookies, many songs and a gypsy band. The English doctors gave each man and woman a cigarette and a pair of socks. All are very happy. The woman smoke more than the men here, I believe, and our Russian sisters smoke all the time. They think we are awfully queer. The English sisters all smoke too.

This noon I saw a poor thin boy of sixteen with one arm off and a side all torn up. He suffered so when he was being dressed I gave him a cigarette. He was delighted and passed it all around to his friends for a puff. They are the bravest and most lovable sort of boys. It makes my heart ache. We have one of eleven years with an arm off. Everyone in this tiny country has done his bit to save the land of Roumania and I fear all in vain.[20]

October 14, 1917

We had a very busy day and I was just cleaning up the operating room to go to dinner at 8 p.m. when we were notified that 300 patients had arrived at the station by hospital train and our ambulance would bring them to the hospital. We tore around like mad getting the operating room ready as every case must be dressed before being sent into the wards. We put cots up in the halls and stretchers and boxes and piles of straw, etc. then along came only five patients and we cannot locate where the rest are. They came in on the train and say that others are coming. They may not show up until to-morrow night. The transportation is a terrific problem. Probably two hundred or three hundred will be dead. If our staff ever gets through Russia, we will have two hundred auto ambulances and we can get right to the front and remove the wounded quickly.

Russia is a terrible problem. They will not fight. The English have sent many guns and the minute they think the Germans are near they retire. They have no strong leaders. The people are drunk with their freedom and will not take orders from anyone. One of our men saw a Russian stabbed and dumped into an ally the other day. He probably tried to get something done. If an officer gives an order, the men vote on whether they will obey or not. No one works, no one is responsible. Some of the best Russians are terribly distressed, but helpless, they are so overpowered by the great number of ignorant peasants, who really want the Germans to get control of Russia because they could get beer or vodka. No wonder they cannot. They know so little and their country has done so little for them they cannot see why they should fight for it.

The Roumanians have all decided to leave the trenches on October 15ᵗʰ (tomorrow) and go home. We do not know but we fear there are really two Germans on this line. If we had a few Americans here, we could do something, but the Germans treat the Russians well and we fear a separate peace is very near. If so, we will be closed in unless Russia signifies that we can be shown to the coast and you can bet we will pick up our heels. We do not care to be German prisoners. They would probably put us to work in their hospitals.

Everything is quaint and so old-fashioned here. For instance there is in our tower which forms the entrance to the hospital a big bell which rings at the most unexpected times and we noticed a pounding noise each time before it rung. Upon inquiring into it was found that it is quite necessary to pound all around the bell with great big sticks for fifteen minutes to drive the devils away before they rung the bell. Poor little picturesque Roumania is almost gone. Before the war they thought of little but pleasure, mostly dress and powder. They say the officers of the army all painted and powdered and wore corsets but now they have changed and are very businesslike. They are quite a capable people and it is very interesting to know that at the Officer's Headquarters where we eat only three out of the seventy-two officers were in the army before. The rest were lawyers, musicians, artists and some business men. Everyone went into the army to save their country, even young boys. You very seldom see a man not in uniform. It makes you very anxious to help them. They are doing their best and they fight very well but have such a short line and the Russians gave way to the north.[21]

The High Command of the Roumanian Army
National Geographic Magazine, Sep 1916, photograph from general staff,
Roumanian Army

Katherine described a dog fight between two airplanes, as witnessed overhead during the middle of the day, in her next letter home. It must have been an amazing sight to witness an airplane combat so close. The Red Cross Unit saw a lot of action, even though they were set back from the fighting front line.

October 26, 1917

> You would laugh if you could see me sitting under a lovely old apple tree overlooking a wonderful valley of forests and a quaint little gypsy town in the far distance the Carpathian mountains are blue and white topped. All is exquisite now in autumn colors. I can scarcely believe there is a war and so near. I had a touch of ptomaine poisoning last night so was told to remain in bed today. I feel all right however and just escaped from my room to wander here. All is quiet and very peaceful now but yesterday it was very different. About 10 a.m. we heard guns starting on all sides and we stopped everything

and ran outside to see a battle in the air directly over our heads. A German aeroplane and a Roumanian plane fought for a long while circling around each other. Then the Roumanian plane came down and from the mountains on all sides guns sent forth little balls of smoke toward the German visitors. After a while the sky seemed polka dotted with little white puffs. Some of them seemed to get quite near the aeroplane which flew around quite as unconcerned as a bird and managed to drop two bombs directly into our peaceful little town. One was no good and the other did a little damage to the railroad station. There is no fighting now and all is very quiet. We are quite bored by the silence and lack of new patients. However, it is very cold today and that means typhus fever will start soon and we will have all we can do. Contrary to the usual custom in these warring countries where all go to the army, the civilians suffer extremely. We want to do just as much as we can for the mothers and children and if our ship ever comes in, we will be in position to help a great deal.

We were quite surprised to see an American boy of twenty-one years appear at our door the other day in a German uniform and say he had heard Americans were here so he had escaped to come to us. He lived in Chicago eighteen years, his father and mother being Germans, so he enlisted when the war started. But recently he heard that America was at war with Germany, so he determined to be with America. The Roumanians here are most suspicious of him, but he is just a typical, adventuresome, good looking, sharp American boy and seems straight as anyone. He says few Germans in the trenches know that America is in the war, that the German soldier is confident of the final and early victory, that they are well fed with half a pound of meat each day and good food of all kinds. He was sent out with a group of men to do propaganda work in getting the Russians and Roumanians to leave the trenches so he was able to escape. He told us some of the work along the line and it was most interesting. We are expecting every day to hear that the Russians have all left the trenches and that they have made separate peace. That would of course be the end of Roumania and we would leave as fast as possible. This existence is terrible. This coarse black bread and cabbage is getting too frequent. No milk, eggs, butter, white bread, meat, fats of any kind or sweets. You have no idea how we miss it and how hard hardtack is. If we were able to do a lot of great work we would not care but when we have a hospital full of convalescents who are slowly starving to death and unable to resist the poisoning from their infected wounds. I tell you it makes us all terribly blue. We are here, but our hands are tied. We are suffering hardships to no avail. We would not care about what we get if we could only do more. That is the hard part but not a word from our supplies. We don't know where they are. Dr. Kirkpatrick I believe is quite determined that we will not stay if we cannot get wood to heat the hospital or food to feed the patients. These last letters all must seem like general complaints but things are really pretty bad. We have no bandage, no gauze, no medicine. We lack everything to start in the winter with and all because Russia is in such a state that they hold up or confiscate all supplies and we have no other way of getting them. If our supplies would only come we could plan to start several hospitals for typhus and do a great deal of work in the home and for the people. They are suffering enough already and need all the hope to give them.[22]

Katherine wrote to her Cousin Anna about how the unit coped with the shortage of supplies and some of the hardships of the war. "Katherine told of the bandages sometimes made of newspaper tied on with straw, operations carried on without anesthetics, the discovery of a "dead village" in which all the adults had died of typhus, leaving hundreds of helpless children to be rescued and cared for."[23]

In her next letter home, Katherine described the local population and the gypsies who dwell across the lands.

Roumanian Gypsy Women
*National Geographic Magazine, Feb 1917, Frederick
Moore*

October 27, 1917

Took a long walk into the country today. It is really
fascinating. You know Roumania is the original home of the
gypsies and that we have some tribes in America. The peasants
here are all gypsies. I have taken many pictures and will try to
send you some if I can get them printed. I am also trying to
buy some fine homespun linen. It is really great but since the
war most of it has been used up. It seems terrible not to get any
letters. We expect they will all come in a bunch when they do
come. Mail will be sent at regular intervals from the legation
here in Jassy by a special carrier, a man who carries a bag of
diplomatic mail straight through America. We will send letters
each time such a carrier goes. I am not sure yet how often that
will be it has been very quiet here lately, no fighting. Don't
think there will be much until spring. Fever is starting now
which will keep us busy.[24]

Katherine wrote to her cousin Anna regularly during World War I. This next insight written to Anna, discussed where the unit was living, their plans to survey the conditions in surrounding areas and the difficult environment in which they worked.

Reporting on the last months of their stay in Roumania, when the unit had been ensconced in an old hospital of large size, Katherine wrote: I have just started an out-patient department. The people need it so much and it will also give me more insight into the civilian life. I am going out tomorrow to visit the schools and inspect the children, bringing them to the clinic if they need it. A young Russian doctor is coming with me as he speaks English as well.

There are countless refugees. Quite a number of refugee girls are helping around the hospital and the Boy Scouts are generally helpful. I went out this morning to look up a badly burned baby who had not been brought back to the hospital and I found a family of six children under ten, the father a prisoner in Germany, the mother evidently ill with typhus. Every child was stark naked, huddling beside a queer little plastic stove: typhus evidently does not take the children. They had had only a few half cooked beans for days. Then when one of the doctors and I visited some of the orphanages we also found frightful conditions-conditions existing all around us. We have taken out bundles of clothes to families and suppose we are actually doing some good: but there is so much we can't touch. If we can only get supplies and food from Russia! With the cruel lack of everything-so short of medicines, gauze, cotton, etc. when we think of the mass of supplies shipped by the American Red Cross in vain, we feel like killing!

We are living in a huge corridor affair in one wing of the hospital, as it is not safe to live outside the hospital. In the evenings we play cards if we can get warm enough; usually we are so sold and hungry that we crawl into our straw bunks and forget everything as soon as possible.[25]

Suddenly, the Red Cross Unit's work was disrupted by the war erupting around them. Letters home were entrusted to a courier, as departure was imminent. Katherine's letter sounded calm, but must have been hastily mailed before leaving. William T. Ellis enclosed a note with each letter from the unit, reassuring families at home.

December 10, 1917

When leaving Roumania, last month (Nov 1917), I was entrusted with a large budget of letters by members of the American Red Cross Mission to Roumania, and by Mr. Morgan, of the YMCA, among them being one addressed to you. I could bring these letters only as far as Liverpool, owing to war regulations.

So I am writing this memorandum to assure you of the good health and spirits of all the Americans. And also to inform you, in confidence, that they were not caught unprepared by the recent collapse of Russia, which isolates Roumania. Complete arrangements had been made for the secure and independent exit of all the Americans, as soon as it should become necessary. Naturally, I cannot write in detail of the plan, but I wish to give my personal assurance that the safest persons in all the Russian sphere today are the Americans in Roumania.

Aside from the letters I carried, being the last man out, you may not hear again for some time, but all is well, none the less.

William T. Ellis [26]

Katherine's note was delivered to the Liverpool, England post office by William T. Ellis.

Jassy, Roumania
November 1917

Dear Mother, Almost started for home tonight. Things are getting quite close here and I can assure you, mighty interesting. The armistice and actions of the Russians make it almost certain that we will have to leave here very shortly and so we were all packed up to pull out on the evening train, when we discovered that the trains could not move, owing to the lack of coal. We are bunking tonight in a large office building used by us while distributing supplies to the people. We finally were able to get a good deal of clothing and food through Russia and the men have been quite busy getting it distributed over the country before we had to get out.

I wish I could tell you all the exciting things that happen each day, but I can when I get home. We are now planning a wild scheme to go down to Persia and start a hospital right at the front, under tents. Our usefulness here is at an end; if Russia and Roumania make peace and we will have to get out, and get out quickly too. All the Roumanian doctors will come back from the front then, so we will not be so badly needed anyway.

Our trip to Persia will be great and adventurous." We will go by train to the Caucasian mountains and then for nineteen days any way (I don't know how many miles it is), we will have to go in automobiles, if we can buy some in Russia, if not on camels down to where the English troops are fighting so bravely against the Turks, about five miles now they say from Jerusalem. We would have a long, exciting trip, at least three months to get there from here. Of course, we don't know for sure whether we can get there or not, all we know tonight is that we can't stay in Roumania, because when they, make peace, they are our enemies, or practically the same, and yet so far we cannot get out of here because they are fighting so much in 'Russia and to get out of Russia either by the way we came through Siberia or by the Atlantic we must go to Petrograd, and that is impossible, right now.

Things may clear up and because of the dangers of Persia we may come home, most likely again by Siberia, which makes a two months trip, so all is so very uncertain and things change here so rapidly. We may go to an entirely different place tomorrow.

It is really great fun here. We are all well and having such jolly times in all the excitement. Four of us came up in an ambulance day before yesterday to clean up and start a new hospital in Jassy. We got to work scrubbing up, had about twenty Roumanian men working at it like mad, moving hospital supplies over from the storeroom and getting more or less settled, when suddenly last night we were told at 6 p. m., that we must have all our stuff packed and out ready to leave at nine the next morning, that the soldiers were returning from the front to protect the king and that 2,000 men would be put in that building. Maybe we didn't do some scrabbling – all our own things to pack, as we expected to leave for Petrograd immediately – but after we were all out the trouble loomed up so we can't get off. The soldiers are coming in tonight and we are, I must admit, glad to be rid of the building for a hospital. It was built I believe, for a palace for the king, but he chose another. It is a wonderful, big white castle affair, huge and cold, no heating but those little white washed stoves and of course no bathrooms, they are unheard of here.

Well, another day and all is quiet here. We four nurses slept very well in the colonel's office and outside the barred windows a huge man with a long bayonet on his gun tramped up and down all night. We felt exactly like jail inmates, but right next door a few hours after we got our trunks and things out, a thousand soldiers marched in and we watched them. In the morning it was quite a scene, columns of quiet men with bayonets glistening, followed by huge cannons and columns of ammunition. This morning we are surrounded by soldier's camp fires, wagons and guns, but they are all peaceful and happy so far. Just from the trenches, so sleeping on the cold, bare floors of the huge old building, under cover, is quite luxury to them. We are of course not at all sure why so many soldiers came in the night. We hear tales of every hue, massacre of all the Jews here is one. They hate the Jews and there are many here, so we wait. Peace is another. Retreat is another. We will know perhaps by night; perhaps not. At present we are practicing "watchful waiting". I am as usual without ink in my fountain pen, so hope you can read this. I will get ink when the secretary comes.

We have just heard that 20,000 soldiers are mobilizing here. The streets are full of men. We know not what is up, but it looks thrilling. We are waiting for things to develop and they seem to be coming to a head rapidly. Dr. Perkins is starting out in a short while to try to get to America with some important letters, so I am sending a note to you, asking him to carry it as it seems our only way to get mail through. I am all right, well and flourishing on the excitement. I wish I could run in and tell you all the exciting things we are seeing and doing. It surely is great and if we can get do to Persia, we will have a most wonderful trip. We are taking lots of good pictures and hope we can get home with them. We are safe and happy, so don't worry about us.

Your loving daughter, Katherine[27]

The resourcefulness of the Red Cross Unit was acknowledged for the work they accomplished in Romania in spite of lack of supplies by Davison. He described their achievements during the winter months in the following excerpt.

The winter was now at its height, but the clothing problem had been relieved. From various places in Russia, the Commission had secured material, thread, needles, buttons and sewing machines. The Red Cross Canteen at Jassy was operated in connection with public triage – a bathhouse and disinfector; and having cleaned, fed and restored to animate interest in life, thousands of women were set to manufacture simple clothing. Thousands of garments were manufactured, the Queen herself distributed many of them in small country villages. The records show that at the relief station in Jassy where now food, clothing, disinfection and medical attention were dispensed, 1200 persons were cared for daily from the date of its opening on February 25, 1918 to March 9, 1918 when the Commission was forced to leave Rumania by the imposition of the German peace.[28]

Cousin Anna provided an interesting description of Queen Marie of Romania's reaction when the war situation escalated. "Poor heroic Queen Marie, heart-broken, was eager to help. She told her friends about two automobiles, the gift of an American admirer, hidden away with barrels of benzene sunk into the earth beside them-barrels which, upon investigation, proved to be empty. The unit had become caught in the Russian Revolution and had to make an escape."[29] Benzene is a chemical solution used in production, but may have been used as a type of fuel for automobiles. Cars were not prevalent at this time and there were no gas stations in Romania in 1918.

And when the final day arrived, "On March 9, 1918 to save herself from utter annihilation by Germany, Rumania gave up the struggle. Russia, her former protector, had played her false in practically the last political act before she herself went down into an abyss of revolution and Bolshevism."[30]

When departure of the Red Cross Unit was imminent, the Queen's response was documented by a cable to Red Cross Headquarters in Washington, D.C.

At the time of the Mission's departure, Rumania's Queen cabled to Washington as follows: At this hour when tragic events leave my country defenseless in the hand of a revengeful and relentless enemy, my thoughts turn with gratitude towards those who in anxious days, but when there was still hope, came to my aid. I wish once more to thank the American Red Cross for the splendid way in which they answered my appeal of a few months ago. The work the American Red Cross Commission did amongst our wounded and amongst the suffering population is unforgettable to me and my people. Now that my country has to remain alone and forsaken, surrounded by foes, I wish to raise my voice and to thank all those who helped me, and to ask that we and our nation should not be forgotten, although a dreadful and humiliating peace has been forced upon us. I ask of the great heart of America to remember Rumania, if even for a while. Strangulated, her cries will not reach it, and her tears will have to be wept in secret.

To the thoughtless, it might appear that the Red Cross' mission in Rumania was a failure. But even these persons, would not say so had they been among the fortunate ones who were present when Marie of Rumania conferred decorations on the members of our Mission. All of them have since said that they knew that the decorations were the only proofs of her gratitude the Queen has left to give, but it was easy to see that she exulted in the giving.[31]

Barbee Cross
presented to Katherine Olmsted by Queen Marie of Romania

**Johns Hopkins University, Sheridan Libraries
and Museums**

"The iron barbee/arrow cross is engraved with a crown on the front, suspended from an oval rind to be attached to a ribbon. Inscription on the back reads "1917" engraved."[32]

6

Escape from the Siege 1918

The Red Cross Unit had to attempt escape from a German led siege of Romania. An interesting description of the situation, as experienced by the nurses and doctors first hand, was recorded by Katherine through letters to her cousin and an exclusive interview with the Record local newspaper after arriving home. An excerpt from Anna Olmsted's booklet reads;

The activities of the mission which had begun in September 1917 were forced to come to an end in March 1918, when the Germans ordered the American, French and British agents of relief from the country. Immediate flight was necessary, but how to escape alive was the question. As Katherine wrote in a letter from Roumania, "We have at present little hope of getting out, with enemies on all sides. For over ten days now the Russians and the Bolsheviks have been fighting only about twenty miles away and have destroyed communication through Russia. We are between two fighting fronts and probably are seeing more thrilling things than many of the nurses who are over fifty miles from the front.

"We get a scare-the Germans are coming-the Bolsheviks are coming-or other startling news brought by apparently reliable messengers-and we start packing up. Then the news is contradicted. Once we were packed ready to try to get to Persia (later renamed Iran) when, to our disgust, we were told that it was not safe to go through Russia-so back we came.

"We realize that the Germans would not hesitate to shoot us-that our Red Cross uniforms are no protection. We can't get through Russia or escape to Russia now as there are no trains-and we have not been able to find any automobiles. We have nothing to eat but starches. We are on our last can of coffee which breaks our hearts: we still have a very limited supply of tea and potatoes which we got from the Russian Red Cross, but thank heaven the beans are almost gone!"[1]

In an interview with the Sodus Record after she was safe again at home, Katherine described the first steps the Red Cross Unit took to escape.

When it was announced that Roumania would make peace with Germany, many of the officers were so ashamed that they committed suicide. We had a number of cases in our hospital. After peace was declared the big problem was for our unit to escape with our lives. We knew the Germans would not hesitate to butcher us. The Roumanians and Russians were scrapping at the north and the Roumanians and Germans were having a skirmish on the eastern shore. It looked as though we would have to tunnel through to China or swim the Black Sea. We really expected to return by the way of Persia, but the Germans captured all the trains, so we had to give up this idea. We kept packed up ready to start on a moment's notice. Finally, at eleven o'clock one night the Major, who had been up to Jassy, where we kept our supplies because it was nearer the railroad and because they could get into Russia more easily in case they had to get out, announced that the French would leave the next morning for the north. The unit was ready and started out for the place the train was to leave, a distance of sixty versts. We accompanied the French, British and Italian missions, who had been sent too late to try to offset the German propaganda on the east front.

There were about twelve hundred in the party-all determined to take the risk of getting out. They traveled in the ambulances part of the way and partly on foot until the place of embarkation was reached-and they saw the train! Always leery of the Germans, they hoped to board the train and escape the notice of the roving bands from the German Army. The French Military Mission had been collecting cars for some time. When there was a sufficient number to make up six trains, it was agreed to start on the perilous journey. Each one of us was furnished with a rifle and a revolver. The cars were about like freight cars. Shelves were built on the sides and we used our blankets for bedding. The car we had was the best of those used, but considered a fifth rate affair. When we started out, the French announced that they were ready to fight their way through. The railroads in Russia are in a dreadful state. There are no trains running on schedule. An engineer who had a locomotive, say a year ago, is still running it, providing it has not gone to pieces. He starts out with his engine and runs on any track that suits his fancy, or as occasion may require. The railroad conditions are absolutely in a chaotic state.[2]

The escape trains were a curious setup, as described by the New York Times. "The train on which the Americans traveled was one of the most extraordinary combinations of railway rolling stock ever seen-the engine dated back to 1876 and only burned wood. Each train was provided with food for a month-food cooked in military kitchens abandoned by Russian troops."[3]

A similar wood burning train, Central of Georgia #8, is located at the Georgia State Railroad Museum, Savannah, GA. It was built in 1886 by the Baldwin Locomotive Works and has a wood burning engine."[4] The old fashioned wood burning train is very similar to the one used by the Allies to escape.

1886 wood burning engine, Central of Georgia, Georgia State
Railroad Museum
Photo by Pamela Lee

Anna Olmsted, Katherine's cousin, shared an excerpt from Katherine's letter describing the scanty food situation and vacillating escape directions dictated by local hearsay with the German army on their tail. Imagine approximately 1,200 Allies escaping in six trains, with no clear route and continual changes to avoid capture or worse.

"The food situation was critical. We took what supplies we had left and the French gathered together what they could find.

Our soldiers broke into a car and found some rice and macaroni that had been left by the Russians. The supplies were pooled and divided fairly, although there was very little for each portion.

"When our train started, those in command did not know in what direction, we would go. The Germans were in or near Odessa and we had to keep away from that territory. Orders would be given for the trains to run to a certain point, where investigations were made as to the direction to be taken. The soldiers, would leave the trains and march into a town to ascertain where the German soldiers were. Our direction depended entirely upon what information they secured. We left the vicinity of Odessa about eight hours before the Germans reached that city. They reached a number of places right after we had left. "We have been told that everything was being bombed-in fact we were on a French bombing train-and, as we passed, bridges and anything that might be of use to the Germans were blown up."[5]

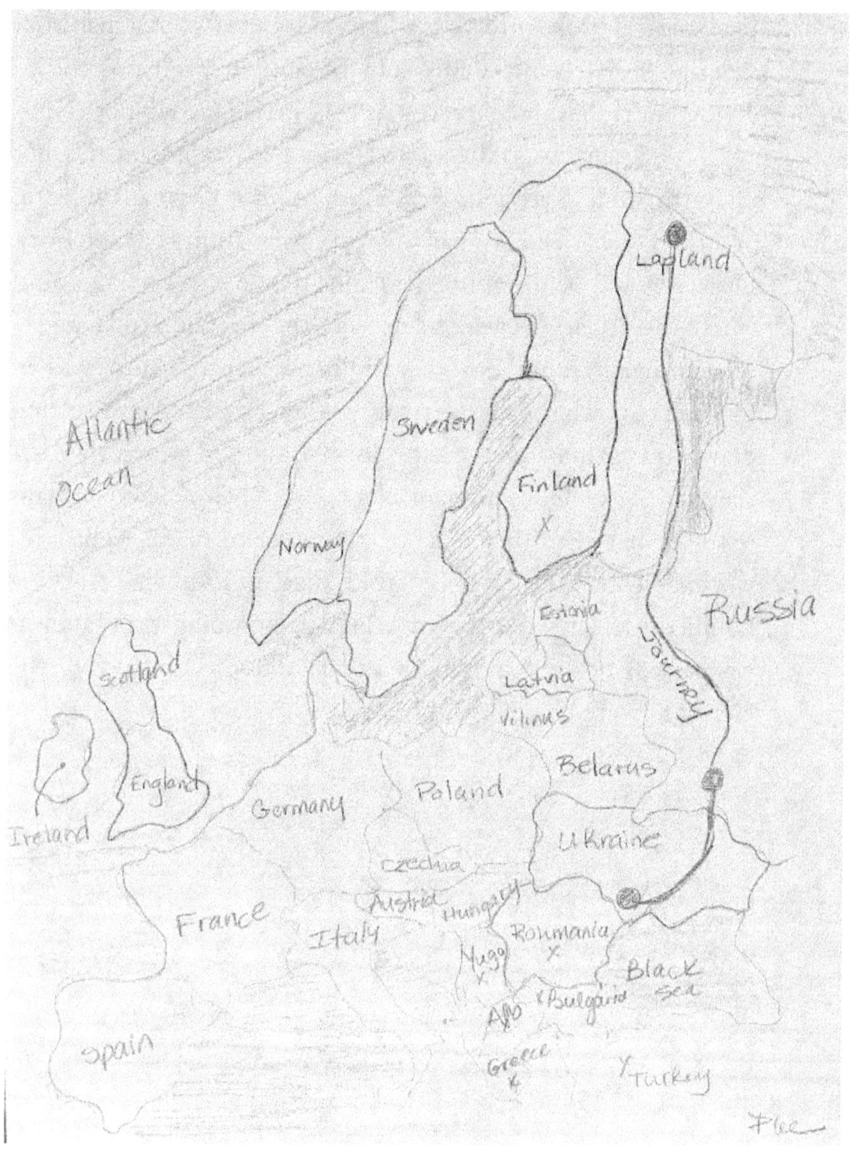

Map from Odessa to Murman Coast
Sketch by Pamela Lee

The Allies escaped past the area of Odessa and were quite near Moscow, a large Russian city. In an interview with the local paper after arriving home, Katherine recounted what their group experienced at various stops on the escape route.

When we reached the vicinity of Moscow we found that anarchy prevailed. Men were being shot down in the main streets. A few of us were venturesome enough to enter the city, although we did not make our way through the principal streets, where so much blood was being shed.

Moscow is typical of Russia as a whole, it is desolate. It is impossible to buy food or clothing.

Ignorance is the principal trouble with Russia to-day. The Bolsheviks are anarchistic. When the leaders of this organization decided that they would have a German peace, they had hundreds of the brave Russian officers shot. 600 officers were assassinated one day and their bodies thrown into the sea. Many thousands of the intelligent citizens were also murdered.

When our trains would reach centers of population they would be surrounded by bands of Russians carrying guns and banners bearing inflaming propaganda. Apparently they would have murdered us upon the slightest provocation but some of our officers could speak Russian and they would alight from the cars and appeal to the crowds, using mild language and keeping in good humor. The Russians would quickly lower their guns and banners and shortly would shriek and applaud the speakers. On the other hand, when we stopped at Kursk we were enthusiastically received by crowds of Bohemian troops who had been prisoners of the Germans.

The trouble with Russia is the lack of leadership and the fact that there are too many I W W's there. If the United States could only send over a number of strong leaders it seems probable that much could be done toward bringing Russia to her senses. Some of the Russian leaders told us that they were getting enough of the Germans; that the Germans were trying to make them stop fighting.

The Russian troubles since the Germans entered Russia, following the peace pact have been much greater than they were under the czar.

Dr. Davidson of New York, a member of our unit, made such progress in his changing of the ideas of the Russians who gathered around our trains at the various stopping points, became so enthusiastic over what he was accomplishing that he decided to remain behind, believing that he could do a splendid work in converting Russians to the idea that the Allies cause was the proper one to support.

What they need is good leaders. They are just like a big bunch of children.

We were particularly anxious to ascertain the feelings of the Russians in reference to the possible intervention of the part of Japan. We had learned that there was some talk of intervention by the Japs in order to protect the supplies in Siberia, so they would not fall into the hands of the Germans. We were informed that the Russians hate the Japanese; that it is the only country that they will fight.[6]

Amidst war and facing seriousness of a life or death situation, sometimes comes acknowledgment and commitment. Taking action when one may have remained silent in other circumstances. There are two brief excerpts referencing the commitment of Katherine and an unnamed American doctor. The two excerpts are summarized together as follows. "By the time they left Moscow, Katherine had become engaged to one of the American doctors. On the journey out of Moscow, the dreary days of exposure to bitter cold and too little food took their toll. Illness spread through the group and two or three doctors died along the way, one of them Katherine's fiancé. And among her possessions was a small blurred photograph depicting a pitiful funeral service conducted on a desolate, windswept Siberian field. She always kept that snapshot someone took of the small burial service on the bleak Siberian plain."[7] The loss of Katherine's American doctor is not mentioned again, but it must have weighed heavily on her heart, as witnessed by her possession of the snapshot.

With no time to grieve the loss of their comrades, the group continued northward. Katherine described the tenuous train tracks and a bombing attack the Allies endured. This segment of the escape route took them just north of Moscow.

For the first hundred miles or so the trains carrying the Allied Missions traveled over a new railway which had been completed only a short time before by Russian military engineers. It was rather a circuitous route, but it was believed the Germans were ignorant of its existence and that it was safer than the old line. It was known that the journey likely would be a dangerous one (each nurse was provided with a rifle and revolver). On the second day, about 200 miles north of Odessa, a flash of fire was seen on the horizon. It was followed by a loud explosion and a great geyser of earth and rocks as a shell burst in a field about half a mile from the moving train, followed by many others, the bombardment continuing for five minutes. The range was a little too great for the German guns, however, and the shells fell short.

Katherine wrote: "That five minute bombardment seemed like hours-the relief was immense when it was over. Along the way other squads of Germans attacked our train several times, shattering windows and inflicting a few wounds-our soldiers returning fire. As a memento of this I have a velour hat with a bullet hole in the crown-good luck this was hanging on a nail in the car while I was lying safely on the floor!"

At a point farther north many members of the Allied Missions left the train, while the others drove back to Moscow. The Revolution was still raging, with the horrible sight of men and women crucified on doors and walls. It was said that any man wearing a clean collar or any well-dressed woman was suspect and might be shot; and no officer dared wear insignia or any mark of rank. Ignorant peasants wanted to kill anyone who could read and write. The Americans, dressed as if they were shabby peasants, wandered about the city seeking a way out. No railroad was available. The money given them by Kerensky was worthless-nothing could be gotten except by barter and clothing was bartered for food.[8]

7

Lapland Safety Point

Katherine continued her interview with the Sodus Record and discussed the original escape route versus the actual next leg of the journey taken. The group decided to travel to Lapland, Murmansk which is north of the Arctic Circle.

Originally the party decided to go to Petrograd, if possible. However it was found that this was impossible. The port in that vicinity was frozen. We found that we could make our way to Murmansk. The Gulf Stream passes near that point and the port there was open because of the influence of the warmer waters. We were not certain how we would reach that point; but the understanding was that the trip would have to be made on sleighs. By chance in a tea room another 'peasant' told us in English (he was Canadian) where we might find a little railroad tracks which had been built by the English-a narrow gauge railroad track leading to Lapland, Murmansk.[1]

**Murman Coast territory through which runs the New Murman
Railway**
National Geographic Magazine, Feb 1917 A.H. Bumstead, Cartographer

Remember the similar wood burning train, the Central of Georgia #8? Anna Olmsted tells of how "the passengers served as engineers, with Katherine taking her turn at the throttle and the nurses even helped to cut wood. The unit ran this special train themselves, thru Siberia to Lapland."[2] The picture of the Central of Georgia's train controls is similar in set up to what the passengers learned to use.

1886 wood burning engine controls, Georgia
State Railroad Museum
Photo by Pamela Lee

Katherine described "the railroad track, which was in very poor shape as the ties were not as numerous as they should have been and only an occasional spike was driven to hold the rails down. The banks of ice were so near the rails that pieces of the cars and the steps were torn out. The windows were also smashed when they came in contact with the ice."[3]

However, the group persevered and Katherine discussed the conditions and how the Allies survived, as her interview with the Record continued.

As we proceeded northward, the cold became intense. All of the women had their feet frozen, as there was no heat aboard the train. After it was discovered that we were suffering so from the cold, the Yankee Ingenuity of some of the men was brought into play. They gathered pieces of iron and tin along the railroad and in one of the villages found a large number of tin cans. The iron and pieces of tin were made into a stove and the tin cans were used for a chimney. The stove and chimney were held together by bits of wire, string and adhesive plaster from the first aid kits. On this stove was done the washing and what cooking there was.

"While enroute through Russia we found it was impossible to secure any articles by the offering of money. The natives were suspicious of all money offerings. Germany and those who were at the head of the revolutionary government in Russia were printing money as fast as the presses could turn it out. The Russians wanted something tangible when they disposed of any article. We knew it would be extremely cold in the northern part of Russia as well as on the ocean, so we traded some of our clothing for fur hats. At the end of our railroad journey it was ascertained that a Russian had killed a reindeer. We traded six pairs of rubber boots, such as the nurses wore, for a piece of the reindeer. If we had only had plenty of sugar and tobacco, we could have gotten wonderful furs. Some of the men had saved cigars and they got reindeer skins and whole hides for a couple of cigars.

"The Germans have been mightily fooled in reference to the crops in southern Russia. The French circulated throughout Roumania that 1915-1916 cereal crops had not been touched. This made the Germans extremely anxious to get to the seat of supplies. A large number of German soldiers were sent to southern Russia to start the booty toward the central powers. When they reached there they found they had been duped. From all we could hear, there is very little grain in southern Russia. The large landowners, who are assigned vast tracts of soil to till, have left the farms to argue the question of rights. Many others are unable to get seed. So the outlook for a good harvest in southern Russia is slim.[4]

Katherine told the Sodus Record of the Allies arrival in Murmansk, incredibly far north, above the Arctic Circle, and of their encounter with the native people.

The road is built on marshland-can only be used in winter when it is frozen. As this is a warm winter the (train) bed was soft, so we rolled around like tops, expecting each minute to be the last. Finally we reached Murmansk, 150 miles above the Arctic Circle. Never shall I forget our first glimpse of the fur-clad little Laplanders. They looked like animals with eight or nine legs-the 'legs' accounted for by fox tails fastened over red leggings to the bottom of skirts. They did not speak any language we could understand-they knew nothing of the war-but they knew the Red Cross and what the Red Cross meant, and were so friendly and overjoyed to see us. They had no fire-wood was scarce and treasured-ate reindeer meat raw and raw dried fish (like dried beef). But reindeer meat frozen in squares and hung on a string tasted marvelous![5]

Two champion reindeer teams and their Lapland owners
National Geographic Magazine, Feb 1917 Natalie Lohositsky

Two married ladies of Lapland with tall hats, debutantes in scarves
National Geographic Magazine, Feb 1917 Natalie Lohositsky

Katherine later told the Record reporter of the unit's deteriorated physical condition upon arrival in Murmansk and of a special surprise she received when venturing into the Murmansk general store.

At the end of ten weeks when we arrived at Murmansk. We were in a serious physical condition—the party as a whole. Each lost many pounds of flesh. Every bone in our bodies ached and we could hardly crawl from our shelves to leave the trains. Our complexions were as yellow as those of Indians, caused largely from the lack of fruits and vegetables.

I received a special thrill at Murmansk. We went into a store to see if we could get any supplies. In looking up I saw a big box on which was stenciled, 'Evaporated Apples, Charles F Burns, Wayne County, New York'. My heart fairly jumped when I saw the inscription I ascertained that the box contained frozen milk. A large number of strings are placed in the box, the milk is frozen and cut into squares. Persons come for the milk and take it home on a string.[6]

Katherine wrote to her cousin Anna, while waiting in Murmansk. She described the fun they had experiencing a new country.

A young Jewish boy who spoke a mixture of English and Yiddish appeared and told us that the boat which had formerly brought salt to Murmansk twice a year had not been seen for two years. So not knowing when we could get out, we enjoyed rides every morning on sleds, with the driver tickling the noses of the reindeer with a feather in lieu of a whip. They go like the wind, while we hang on like mad and shriek with excitement. We ride around in the day time and stay up most of the night watching the Northern Lights and skies-it is so beautiful. It is not really dark all night. This port is open in the winter on account of the Gulf Stream.[7]

Lapland reindeer sled and passengers
National Geographic Magazine, Feb 1917

Katherine also wrote of the mental anguish while waiting for rescue. It must have been an intense time, but then all of a sudden, rescue was in sight.

> With still no sight of a boat, the unit was forced to remain living on the train for several weeks. This living in a crazy train car without heat has been demoralizing and wearing. It has its sorrows and hardships and homesickness-but it's worthwhile-and it will soon be over. The things I long for most are a china cup to drink out of-a chair instead of a duffle bag to sit on, a bed with sheets, some fresh vegetables and news, news, NEWS! We are crazy for news from home-have had no letters or newspapers since August-and this is April.
>
> I can't think of any war experiences we have not had already, except the submarines-and they are coming. Even submarines will seem mild beside what we have just endured. Finally in desperation we decided not to wait any longer-to try to trek to Norway. So we began getting sleds and reindeer and supplies together. Just as we were ready to start there was great excitement. The little Laplanders dragged us over the ice to a gorge at the Gulf Stream path-and there at the base of the gorge was a boat![8]

Katherine described the rescue boat in her interview with the Sodus Record. It certainly was in poor shape, but beggars cannot be choosers. The questionable vessel got them safely out of the country.

> We were obliged to wait three weeks before we could sail for England. The small boat was once owned by the Germans, and had been torpedoed on two occasions. The vessel was in very bad shape and none of us would have been surprised if she had sprung a leak at any time. This boat was a mine sweeper which was captured in the Mediterranean Sea by the British who had

sent a lot of Russian Jews to Murmansk. These refugees refused to work or fight so England had to get rid of them.

The boat was absolutely filthy after these Russians had left the ship and it took us some time to clean up the vessel for the trip to England. Most of the men had to take quarters in the steerage. The food supplies on the ship were about as limited as those we had during our ten weeks on board the train.[9]

Minesweepers were invented out of necessity during World War I. The common fishing trawler was retrofitted to become a savior of war ships and their crews. The Discovery Channel aired a show describing minesweepers and how they worked.

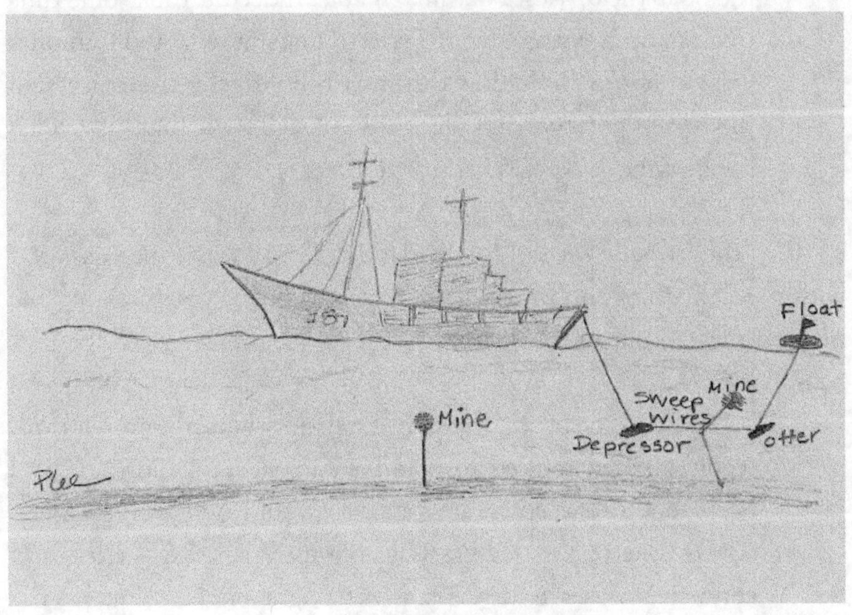

Mine Sweeper
Sketch by Pamela Lee

The Germans had set over 43,000 mines in the English Channel by November 1918. The mines floated and were held down with chains and weights, anchored on bottom of the channel, just long enough to hit the bottom of large sea vessels passing by and would explode when hit. The mines presented a serious danger to war ships. The Allies discovered a way to search and remove the planted mines by use of fishing trawlers especially outfitted, referred to as minesweepers. Fishing trawlers approximately 140 feet long, were steel hulled with shorter depths than war ships. The fishing trawlers were retrofitted with sweep wires that cut the mines free. The mines would then float to the surface and the trawler crew could shoot the mines with guns mounted to the fore and aft, and harmlessly explode the mines.[10]

Katherine described the next steps their group took to make their way home.

> So a hasty swap was arranged: we exchanged our train for the boat-the dirtiest boat imaginable. Indeed it took some time to clean up the vessel for the trip to England. The food supplies were about as limited as they had been on the train-although the frozen potatoes and black rotted cabbage actually provided the best meals we had had in months.[11]

The group finally set sail for England and just when the coast was within reach, they encountered a situation. Thank goodness for the inventiveness of one of the doctors.

> Arriving near land mass in England, the Captain who was feeble-minded refused to take his passengers to port. He had been sent to sweep mines—and he would only sweep mines. At last one of the doctors was able to repair the wireless and contact Newcastle, describing the plight of the refugees. The Captain then was ordered to return to England and seven Zeppelins escorted the boat to the pier.[12]

The total time to escape the siege and arrive in England was approximately two and one-half months. The time line is collaborated by the previously mentioned date March 1918 when the Allies were ordered to leave the country and Katherine's published arrival date in Wallington on May 26, 1918. Although it must have felt much longer to the unit, awaiting rescue.

8

Arrival in London

In an exclusive interview with the Record newspaper, Katherine told of her arrival in England and the surprising response of the unit when they finally reached the land of plenty, comparatively speaking. She also discussed her recovery time at the Red Cross Nurses Club in England.

Our trip to Newcastle, England was devoid of any special excitement. When we landed there, we saw a little girl with a basket of oranges. We made a grand rush for her grabbing the oranges and tossing her coins much larger than the regular price for the fruit. One can hardly imagine the joy we experienced in eating an orange.

As soon as we reached London, we had to go to the police court to secure our food cards before we could get anything to eat. There is no white bread in England except for the sick soldiers. The people are allowed three lumps of sugar a day, one-fourth pint of milk daily and one ounce of meat four times a week.

We were sent to nursing homes for a short stay, to be fed, clothed and rested. While in London, we were entertained at the American Red Cross Nurses' Club. The club is located at the magnificent home of Mrs. Whitelaw Reed, whose husband was a United States ambassador to England at one time. Mrs. Reed donated her home for Red Cross work.[1]

Ambassador Whiteclaw Reid and Elizabeth Mills Reid, Dorchester House, American Embassy, London

theescotericcuriosa.blogspot.com

The lavish manor sits on 8.7 acres of parkland and has an ornamental pond, magnificent specimen trees and woodland walks.

Whiteclaw Reid Manor
dailymail.co.uk, Sept 2023

In the same interview, Katherine also described the war time environment she encountered in 1918 Newcastle, England.

> The women in England are wonderful. They realize the seriousness of the problem. All railroad conductors are women. In all the big railroad stations, there are no men handling baggage, the women are doing all this work. The society women have organized a land army and go out in the country and help the farmers with the crops. It is going to be the making of the women in England. The men respect them more highly than ever. The women are going without everything possible in order that they may send it to France.[2]

According to Katherine's Red Cross Service file, her health was evaluated at the American Nurses Club before being sent home.

> Quality of look – very good, excellent in outpatient and district work and ought not to be used for institutional work for she is quite unusual in her zeal for patients in the home. Conduct – excellent and a most pleasing lecturer. Health – had some intestinal disturbance due to restricted diet last four weeks. Lost over twenty pounds during the year. Miss Olmsted is an unusually loyal and capable woman.[3]

The former American Nurses Club was located at "42 Grosvenor Place, London as stated on the letterhead used for Katherine's medical evaluation, which is today home to Cleveland Clinic at London Hospital" [4]

Katherine summarized her experience thus; "I have traveled entirely around the world, passing through probably twelve countries. I speak some French, German, Russian and Roumanian"[5]

9

Homecoming

The local community recognized Katherine Olmsted as a hero returning from war. Her homecoming interview and picture were plastered on the front page of the local newspaper and took up several pages. And even better than reading about her adventures, the community could listen to Katherine speak about her adventures in person and ask questions at an upcoming live lecture three weeks later.

MISS OLMSTED RETURNS HOME!

Miss Katherine Olmsted, the nurse, who has had such wonderful experiences in Roumania, to which country she went with the Red Cross unit, returned to her home at Wallington Sunday (5/26/1918) to remain with her mother, Mrs. Emma Olmsted, until she has recuperated. Miss Olmsted proved herself 100 per cent patriotic when she resigned a splendid position to make the perilous Journey and to face the privations in faraway Roumania. During the past year The Record published letters received from her by Mrs. Olmsted. Much interest has been manifested in her wonderful experiences in that ill-fated country. The remarkable journey, from Roumania to England recently made by this Red Cross unit attracted world-wide attention. No one knew what had become of that lost Red Cross Unit during their escape. Miss Olmsted granted a Record representative an interview Monday afternoon. In a very charming manner she related her experiences in the war zone.[1]

She said in part: You can imagine my feelings, perhaps, when I saw good old New York. There is no country like America and no place like my home town. It is wonderful to be back and I can hardly realize the terrible experiences we have passed through. I had not received a word from home or seen a New York paper since the 13th of last August. We knew nothing of what had been happening in the States. We were entirely cut off from everything and everybody.

Roumania had to get out of the war. There was nothing left for her to do. The Russians had sent many soldiers into this country. The Roumanians were in desperate straits for food and clothing. They were absolutely starving. The Russian soldiers, who were really of the I. W. W. type, pillaged Roumania. They took everything. The Roumanian soldiers were left without food, and little clothing. They were constantly passing the hospital with very little clothing on. Frequently they did not possess a shirt. Often the soldiers would drop from sheer exhaustion, caused by hunger, and the nurses would pick them up and bring them into the hospital for care. Many of them would die.

It was impossible for the American representatives to get food through to Roumania. The Bolsheviks would seize it and convert it to their own use. Our Red Cross unit had a terrible time getting sufficient food to keep body and soul together. We had no fruits or vegetables of any kind, in fact we did not see any after we left Japan for the trip into Roumania. Horses had to be killed to secure the only meat that it was possible to furnish. Some of the men in our unit had to resort to eating horse flesh. We had no milk, butter, or fats.

While all this was happening, Germany was spreading its propaganda. They bribed a number of the political leaders of Roumania. The king was of German descent. When Russia dropped out of the war, this left poor little Roumania in a dreadful condition. The German propaganda had gotten in its work. The soldiers and civilians were absolutely starving. The political leaders and the king announced that peace with Germany must be brought about. Queen Marie, a most wonderful woman, fairly worshipped by her people, pleaded against a German peace, but to no avail. German propaganda, starvation, and the collapse of Russia led to the peace which has cost Roumania so much. The Germans killed the Roumanian officers and placed Prussians at the head of the regiments. The Roumanians are hoping and praying that the Allies will understand her position. The hearts of the people are with us. "When Queen Marie came to say good bye, the tears streamed down her cheeks. She wanted to return with our unit, as a Red Cross nurse, but she decided to remain behind to see if there was one last chance that she might do her people some good. Queen Marie decorated us before our departure. We have since heard the rumor that she escaped from Roumania and is now in Switzerland.

When asked in reference to the German prisoners who were sent to the Roumanian hospitals, Miss Olmsted stated that in many if not most cases, they were mere boys of from 12 to 18 years old. They did not know for what they were fighting. They were simply told to fight and they obeyed orders. They were nice boys, who knew nothing whatever what the war was about. They were kept in complete ignorance.

Miss Olmsted described her trip across the Atlantic to New York and gave some interesting information relative to the big convoys of ships bearing American soldiers. This information cannot be published owing to government restrictions.

Miss Olmsted stated that all the members of the unit resolved to do everything they could to enlighten the people in reference to Red Cross and war conditions. She has consented to speak of the Red Cross work and her experiences in Roumania at a meeting which will be held at the New Opera House on Sunday night June 16, 1918.[2]

Katherine wrote to Clara Noyes at the Red Cross, "I am extremely glad that it fell to my lot to go with the mission, as it was all a marvelous experience".[3] Although, after such an ordeal, it seemed likely that Katherine needed a rest at home to recover. This was confirmed in her Cousin Anna's booklet; "back in the United States, Katherine spent three months in her grandfather's old home in Sodus, New York, near Lake Ontario."[4] Kathrine remained signed up with the Red Cross reserves, as observed in her Red Cross Service file, however she did not accept any employment offers from them. She received multiple offers of employment by the Red Cross.

On May 31, 1918, Katherine was offered a position for 20 weeks on the Chautauqua Circuit as a Red Cross Representative, to give lectures about the Red Cross. On June 1, 1918 Katherine declined due her health, and she was unable to consider any positions for at least two weeks. She was badly in need of rest. The Red Cross immediately replied and said they could make arrangements in two weeks if she would like to accept the Chautauqua Circuit. Please reply. On June 6th Katherine composed a letter to the Red Cross and stated, "I was sorry not to be able to accept the offer to speak about the Red Cross work on the Chautauqua Circuit as I am so interested in it but since reaching home, I have been quite ill." On this same date, she also sent a telegram to Helen Scott Hay at Red Cross, which said, "Unable to accept your offer. Had to accept permanent position." The position Katherine accepted was with the National Organization of Public Health Nursing.[5]

Katherine gave lectures locally from May 1918 through August 1918, in area towns of Walworth, Lyons and Clyde, New York. Wartime can display the worst of humanity and exhibit a disregard for human life. Atrocious things can be done to people, and having witnessed some of those events, Katherine was not shy about discussing the horrors. What was truly surprising was, The Lyons Republican news reporter printing these gruesome details in the June 14, 1918 edition. The article is not quoted here, however this newspaper can be found online. The news article also states, "Miss Olmsted described the willing sacrifice of the English people as no less than magnificent and thought America might learn a lesson from her brave ally across the sea. Every pound of white flour and sugar in England is being conserved for the use of the soldiers. Even the children refuse to eat white bread and candy for fear of depriving some brave 'Tommy" of the food he ought to have."[6]

World War I was fought in Europe, the poor Brits were close to the frontline and had been members of the Allied Forces for a couple of years before the United States joined in. Based on the U.S. entry into the war later, the local stateside communities may have been slower to respond to the need to conserve food or resources for the troops. Local newspapers reported a large audience attendance at Katherine's lectures. In 1918, most families owned radios but not televisions. Television began to emerge in the 1920s but was not commonplace until the 1950s. I recall visiting my grandparents' home in the 1960s and watching a small black and white television screen housed in a very large box piece of furniture. As described by my grandmother, black and white news reels were played in movie theaters before the feature movie in the early 1900s, especially during wartime. Attending a live lecture and hearing someone's experiences at the war front would have been a thrilling event at that time.

Katherine had an attractive resume with an RN certificate from Johns Hopkins University plus war time experience. She was a sought after commodity and the Red Cross was persistent with job offers.

Miss Minnie Aherns, Red Cross in Washington, noted in Katherine's Red Cross service file on June 25, 1918 that Miss Olmsted has just returned from Roumania and is not very well therefore, not available at present. However, the Red Cross continued to barrage Katherine with employment offers. On July 9, 1918 the Red Cross Director of Bureau Field Nursing Service wrote to request that Katherine keep them informed as to her date of availability for service. Katherine's new employer, the National Organization for Public Health Nursing, sent a request for a special chevron to the Red Cross in an effort to keep her, so Katherine may continue her important work for NOPHN stateside. Although this special chevron was granted, that did not stop the Red Cross from contacting Katherine four times, between October 29, 1918 and November 14, 1918, to request that she join a unit of nurses and doctors traveling to Russia. Katherine declined the Red Cross employment offers.[7]

After declining all employment offers from the Red Cross, the Record announced, "Miss Katherine Olmsted, who has been engaged in lecturing concerning her experiences as a Red Cross nurse in Roumania, has accepted a position in Chicago, where her duties will take her among the children of the city. Her mother, Mrs. Emma Olmsted, will spend considerable time with her during the winter."[8] More information is provided in Katherine's resume. "Katherine accepted a permanent position as Executive Secretary, Central Council Nursing Education, in Chicago, Illinois where she recruited student nurses for a group of seventeen nursing schools."[9] "She also served as Executive Secretary, Western Office, National Public Health Nursing Association at the same time."[10] Katherine was an energetic young lady to serve in two positions simultaneously. She continued to work in the field of nursing, but not as a Red Cross nurse.

The Red Cross Acting Director acknowledged that Katherine's unit had been involved in a siege and agreed that Katherine was not in physical condition to accept a position in Russia or to face a long journey with hardships.

October 29, 1918 from Acting Director, Red Cross Bureau of Public Health Nursing

My dear Katherine, Miss Noyes has handed me the copy of a cablegram received from Dr. Williams which requests Miss Noyes to dispatch several nurses for the Russian Commission. He says in the cablegram "Katherine Olmsted whose public health experience makes her useful for work has told me she could probably obtain release from present duties for service Russia, November. Please communicate directly with her explaining matter and asking her to come."

I have no idea that you are physically able to undertake such a journey or piece of work at this time, and furthermore, think that probably you have your hands full with present position. Nevertheless I must transmit Dr. Williams message to you and ask you to let me know by wire collect, whether you care to consider his proposition.

Personally, I hope you will not consider it as I do not feel that you are in any physical condition to face a long journey and many hardships again and much as I can appreciate this piece of work you might do in Russia, I do feel that we need you here. However, the matter is entirely in your own hands for decision and I shall await your telegram before making any reply.

I do hope you are ever so much better now. Miss Foley wrote me frequently of your condition and at one time seemed considerably alarmed. It is too bad that you had to go through that siege and I hope you will not attempt to do any hard work until you are thoroughly recovered.

Yours affectionately, Acting Director, Red Cross Bureau of Public Health Nursing[11]

Only one response could be made after this letter, and Katherine agreed with the Acting Director. "On November 16, 1918 Katherine sent a telegram to the Red Cross and stated, Extremely sorry, physical condition makes it impossible for me to go to Russia."[12] "Due to her weakened health, Katherine contracted influenza and pneumonia in early October, 1918."[13] "Katherine followed up with two letters on November 19, 1918 explaining in depth why she could not travel to Russia."[14]

It is important to note that Katherine repeatedly declined Red Cross employment offers both in the states and overseas. Understanding her weakened health and perhaps aversion to returning to a war zone, there is one more aspect to consider. "According to a news article in the Record, January 19, 1918, Miss Katherine Olmsted of Wallington resigned a position which was paying her $125 per month as a nurse to enlist as a Red Cross mission nurse in Roumania, at a salary of $60 per month, indicating a patriotism of 100%." The pay rate for a war zone Red Cross Nurse was less than half of what a stateside supervising nurse position paid. The odds were stacked against the Red Cross overseas position, even before the lower pay rate for such a physically dangerous career is considered.

IO

A Series of Misfortunate Incidents

To recap, since returning safely home from the siege in Russia, Katherine took some time to recover in Wallington and continued to speak publicly about her war time experiences locally in upstate New York. Katherine then accepted not one, but two positions simultaneously in Chicago; as Executive Secretary, Central Council Nursing Education and Executive Secretary, Western Office-National Public Health Nursing Association. This is an aggressive schedule for a healthy person, yet in her weakened state the extensive work commitment may have been too much and contributed to her bout with influenza and pneumonia. And then, Katherine became prey to a revenue seeker.

FIRST INCIDENT – ACME LYCEUM BUREAU

At this point, Katherine had spoken about her wartime Red Cross nursing adventure for just over three months in upstate New York. She planned to continue speaking about her war time experiences, but may not have been familiar with venues in Chicago where she now resided. Imagine a sleazy used car salesman type that approached Katherine with glorious visions of handling all booking, promotional and advertising aspects of her speaking engagements. All she would have to do is go and speak. He would take care of the details and she would earn some money. This appeared to be a good proposition for Katherine, who was recovering from influenza and pneumonia. The used car salesman type was actually a representative of Acme Lyceum Bureau, a revenue seeking sensationalist firm that took advantage of an easy meal ticket. The dollar signs must have flashed in his eyes. And to Katherine, help with the coordination of talks may have been very appealing. Okay, it may or may not have happened quite that way, but it is easy to imagine when reading through Katherine's Red Cross service file. Acme was a questionable endorsement name, even mentioned in Bugs Bunny Wile E. Coyote cartoons years later.

On November 29, 1918 Minnie H. Ahrens, Red Cross Chicago, IL sent a telegram to Miss Clara Noyes, Director, Department of Nursing, American Red Cross Washington, D.C. informing her that Katherine Olmsted who was with the Roumanian Unit had accepted an appointment with Acme Lyceum to tell of foreign experience and would also present Red Cross nursing service activities. Would you approve of her wearing the uniform with cape? Please wire answer. On December 2, 1918 Clara Noyes wired the response that she had no objection to Katherine wearing the uniform. However, it was not desirable to urge disenrollment from military camps due to a nursing shortage.[1]

All approval aside, once the American National Red Cross executives saw Katherine's poster and got wind of the sensationalized marketing scheme of Acme Lyceum Bureau, they were not happy. At the end of 1918 the very head of the American Red Cross, National Headquarters, Washington, D.C. Mr. S.M. Greer, discovered Katherine's speaking engagements with Acme Lyceum after he received a copy of the Acme flyer.

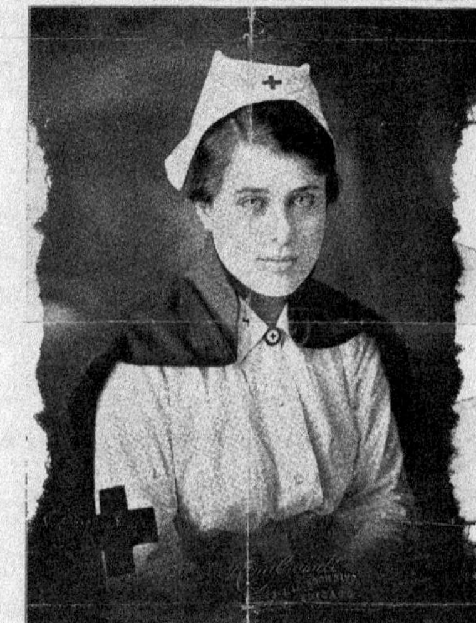

Acme Lyceum Bureau Poster
National Archives file 2 of 2, 120

THE ACME LYCEUM BUREAU

PRESENTS

Miss Katherine Olmstead

(Member of the Red Cross Commission to Roumania)

OF THE

American Red Cross

In Her Absorbing Narative

"My Experiences Amid Roumanian and Russian Chaos"

Through Chaos, Anarchy, Pestilence and Peril As a Red Cross Nurse

THE mere mention of Miss Olmstead's name will be sufficient for the many who have read about her in the Red Cross Magazine and the daily press of the country. As a Red Cross nurse and member of the organization's Commission to Roumania, she embarked from a Pacific port for Vladivostok, Siberia, by way of Japan. They arrived there after the fall of the Russian Czar, and the Krensky government had sent the Czar's own special train to convey them all the way from Vladivostok to Roumania. For days and days they rode, in plush and mahogany, on the finest and most luxurious train in the world, across the vast, sombre steeps of Siberia, down through turbulent European Russia and into Roumania, whose army and population was already flooding back, almost in choatic mass, before the onrushing Hun hordes.

She witnessed the Russian army in Roumania, insane over Bolshevicic falacies, in its wild debacle out of the country, shooting its officers, and crucifying them on trees and barn doors; saw the once proud and prosperous kingdom of Roumania weaken and grow limp as the awful Hun clutches tightened their grip, while whole villages were being wiped out by the deadly typhus fever and thousands of naked children dying from cold and starvation; labored for weeks among the wounded, sick and dying, taking every risk and making every sacrifice; and then, after staying to the last moment, made her way, with the others of the Commission, out through the anarchy of Russia, traveling ten weeks in box cars, across Lapland in sleighs—and back to a world not enveloped by the night of Hun Kultur.

Miss Olmstead graduated from high school in 1906, entered John Hopkins University, where she secured a degree, and before being selected to accompany the Commission to Roumania was connected with the Extension Division of the University of Wisconsin—and at the present time is Secretary of the National Organization (Western Dept.) for Public Health Nursing. She is an experienced public speaker, and tells her story in a sweet, unaffected manner that holds her audiences spellbound from beginning to end. She is a beautiful girl and a beautiful character, modest and friendly, and it is a rare privilege just to meet and know her.

The Biggest Story of Red Cross Work and Experience of the Great World War.

December 30, 1918 an interoffice memo from Howard W. Fenton, Manager to George E. Scott, General Manager, Washington Headquarters states "it would be easier for you to control Miss Olmsted than the Acme Lyceum Bureau. Do not hesitate to communicate directly with Miss Olmsted."[2]

January 4, 1919 S.M. Greer wrote to Miss Noyes and requested information about Katherine Olmsted. January 6, 1919 reply from Miss Noyes – Miss Olmsted is a member of the Red Cross Nursing Service but is not at the present time on active duty. She is a western Secretary of the National Organization for Public Health Nursing. She was a member of the Roumanian unit. Acme should not advertise her as a Red Cross Nurse, as that would imply she was acting for the Red Cross which is, of course, not the case. Miss Noyes will take this up with Katherine.[3]

Clara Noyes, Director, Department of Nursing, wrote to Katherine on January 7, 1919 c/o Acme Lyceum Bureau. She stated, "my attention has been called to the fact that the Acme Lyceum Bureau of Des Moines is advertising lectures given by you featuring you as a Red Cross nurse.

We recognize the value to the Acme Lyceum Bureau advertising you as a Red Cross nurse, but as this would imply that you were actively engaged in this work by the Red Cross it does not seem consistent with our policy to utilize this organization to further the interests of any private enterprise.

I am sure that you will be glad to give me some further information upon the matter as I feel certain that a satisfactory explanation is available. May I ask if you are using your Red Cross Uniform? [4]

Wow, didn't Miss Noyes remember giving permission for Katherine to wear the uniform and speak? Katherine had spoken to Minnie Ahrens in the local Red Cross Chicago office, who gained permission and loaned her the uniform.

On January 12, 1919 Katherine responded, 25% of proceeds goes to the towns. She had already spoken in Essex, Shenandoah and future dates were with clubs, churches, YWCA and theatres. She confirmed that Minnie Aherns, Red Cross, approved and that she loaned her a cape for poster picture. I am not wearing a uniform as I am not on active duty. Katherine asked, "Are you going to prevent the returning Red Cross Nurses from telling their experiences either with lecture bureaus or personally advertised lectures, as of many soldiers and doctors are now?"[5]

January 21, 1919 Miss Noyes replied to Katherine, "I feel sure you will appreciate the point that I am trying to make and will understand that while we do not wish to interfere with personal liberty we must make a very definite effort to protect the use of the Red Cross. Unless these talks were under the joint auspices of the Red Cross and the Acme Lyceum Bureau the speaker should not have been featured as a Red Cross lecturer. Part of our Public Health program during the coming year is to provide nurse speakers in full uniform for a tour of the country. They, however, will be under contract with the Red Cross. There is absolutely nothing to prevent a returning Red Cross nurse from speaking of her experiences but these, however, we believe should be incidental to the main subject presented and not made to appear as a Red Cross feature.

I trust I have made my point clear and feel sure that you will yourself look after the advertising, personally, in the future. **You can readily see how cheap the Red Cross would become if all the twenty-four thousand nurses who are now in service were to blossom out into publicity as returning Red Cross**

nurses. It is our desire to protect our service and the use of the sacred emblem that we have established not only the statutory laws but the moral ones as well.[6]

January 27, 1919 Katherine replied to Miss Noyes; I am very sorry to have caused the Red Cross any uneasiness concerning my lecturing. As the Acme Lyceum Bureau would not reprint literature and posters leaving out the Red Cross emblem, I immediately refused to give any more lectures for them. I found that it was not at all satisfactory to be connected with a profit making agency.[7]

January 29, 1919 – Miss Noyes replied; I felt sure you would see the situation from our point of view. I am wondering however, if the National Organization would release you for one of the Chautauqua Circuits for Red Cross? [8]

Katherine displayed a lot of energy and enthusiasm, although misguided at times. Did Miss Noyes have an ulterior motive when she offered a speaking engagement with the Red Cross? Was Miss Noyes annoyed that Katherine repeatedly turned down offers to speak for the Red Cross, however continued to speak about her nursing adventure on her own, unedited?

A year later there was correspondence from Katherine to Miss Noyes, "I shall be very glad to serve as a member of Miss Ahrens' committee for the purpose of working out a plan for branch headquarters in the central states."[9] The Red Cross was finally successful in channeling some of Katherine's excess energy within their span of control, even if just in a volunteer capacity.

SECOND INCIDENT- ADVERTISING IN RED CROSS MAGAZINE

Katherine keenly felt the shortage of nurses and advocated for new nurses in her lectures, historically requested brochures regularly from the Red Cross, even wrote about the shortage in a pamphlet titled, "the Dearth of Public Nurses."[10]

In the beginning of 1920, Katherine referred two Nursing Correspondent Schools to the Red Cross Magazine Advertising Department. The Chicago School of Nursing office was located in the same building as the office of the National Public Health Nurses where Katherine worked and she admitted to visiting the Chicago School of Nursing. Alice Hood of the Elizabeth McCormick Memorial Fund in Chicago wrote, "I have known of this so-called school for some time and know that it is the cheapest sort of an organization."[11]

Chicago School of Nursing Ad, Red Cross Magazine Dec 1919
National Archives, file 1 of 2, 43

The Red Cross service file is unclear if Katherine sought out these correspondent school agencies with the idea of promoting nursing classes to the public or if the agencies contacted her directly.

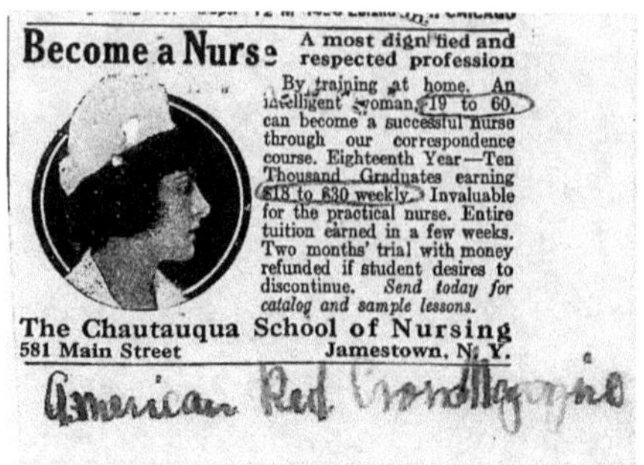

Chautauqua School of Nursing Ad, Red Cross
Magazine Dec 1919
National Archives, file 1 of 2, 45

In any event, Katherine's referrals resulted in two ads published for the Chicago School of Nursing and the Chautauqua School of Nursing in the Red Cross Magazine. Due to written complaints by large donors to the Red Cross, Katherine submitted copies of the ads to Miss Clara Noyes, Washington, D.C. and stated in part, I think that it's a very poor policy, especially in Chicago, to make any public demonstration against these courses which have been conducted for the past 20 years and are training practical nurses. I have visited the Chicago one, and find them frank in their limitations. However, the ads could prove dangerous, if the public believes that the Red Cross sanctions the courses and they could become Red Cross nurses.[12]

Needless to say that Red Cross Headquarters was again upset with Katherine. Miss Noyes, Director of Dept. of Nursing, Washington, D.C. had the advertising suppressed because they were introduced by a new and energetic advertising agent who had lost track of the fact that the Red Cross Magazine accepted no advertising of this nature. Furthermore, the letter dated 3/22/1920 to Katherine stated, there is one statement that you make which I cannot agree with, that these courses do not attempt anything more than a training for practical nurses. It is a most insidious and dangerous movement that persistently interferes with nursing standards, legislation for good nursing laws and advancing the profession. It was a matter of great chagrin to me to find that these advertisements had been introduced into the Red Cross Magazine.[13]

American School of Correspondence Ad and
Haywood Tire & Equipment Company Ad
National Archives, file 1 of 2, 45

Next to these ads in the Red Cross Service file, was a picture of two other questionable service ads from other companies. Apparently, when the service file was scanned in 1978, they scanned both the back and the front of the documents. The back scan included these two advertisements in that same magazine; "High School Course in Two Years, Learn at Home offered by American School of Correspondence, Chicago, U.S.A. and Make $3,000 In One Year Repairing Automobile Tires by Haywood Tire & Equipment Company, Indianapolis, Ind."[14] Apparently, Red Cross HQ Washington was only concerned with suppressing correspondent school nursing class advertisements and accepted other scurrilous advertisements. Included here are the other two ads which were which were not suppressed.

THIRD INCIDENT – REFUSES PRIME POSITION AND GOES WITH CONTENDER

Two and half years after the Romanian siege and escape, and in spite of the mounting incidents, the Red Cross continued to lobby Katherine to work for them. The Acting Director had located a prime employment position and she wanted Katherine to fill it. The only catch, the position was in Europe.

Ida Butler, Acting Director for the Red Cross Department of Nursing wrote to Katherine and let her know that Miss Noyes was in Europe making a survey of public health nursing and training to be done. Miss Noyes had indicated that, "There is a position available as an Assistant to Miss Hay, Chief Nurse of Red Cross Commission to Europe. I hope that Miss Olmsted will be interested. The hardships which she and others endured in Roumania do not exist now. Will you consider this at $3,000 per year without maintenance?" Katherine replied by telegram to Ida Butler on Nov 19, 1920 and indicated she could leave in January, but felt it was impossible to accept less than thirty five hundred without maintenance, as she had responsibilities at home. There was no immediate response and Katherine sent a telegram to Ida Butler again on Nov 30, 1920 stating that she was anxious to know the decision as soon as possible, because she had to secure and train a successor for her present work. Still no response from American Red Cross (ARC). Next item in the service file is a letter from Katherine to Ida Butler on December 15, 1920 informing her that she accepted a position of Director of Public Health Nursing with League of Red Cross Societies (LORCS), in Geneva Switzerland.[15]

In 1921, Katherine Olmsted became the Associate Chief of the Department of Nursing and Director of Public Health Nursing for the League of Red Cross Societies in Geneva, Switzerland. A year later, in 1922, Katherine accepted the position of Director of the Department of Nursing, where she continued Alice Fitzgerald's (Johns Hopkins class of 1906) work to form public health nursing organizations worldwide.[16]

The competitive offer from LORCS may have been prompted through the network of Johns Hopkins Alumnae Nurses. The Red Cross Service file does not have any additional notes on the Assistant position with ARCS, which Katherine declined. Was Miss Clara Noyes miffed because Katherine did not accept the position she was earmarked for at the original salary?

An important item to note is that "Katherine negotiated a salary of $3,500 per year without maintenance as Director of Public Health Nursing with LORCS for her second tour of duty."[17] For Katherine's first tour of duty, no mention of pay rate was made in her service file. It was not until the Sodus Record local newspaper reported upon her return home that she had formerly resigned a nursing position paying her $125 per month and later received a Red Cross salary of only $60 per month.[18] Katherine took care of the salary agreement upfront this time around.

FOURTH INCIDENT – MAKES BIG REQUESTS OF BIG EXECUTIVES a.k.a. MAKES WAVES

While getting ready to leave, Katherine had some loose ends to tie up in her current position as General Federation of Women's Clubs Chairman in Chicago. She wrote to the heads of the American Red Cross and requested that they write brochures so that she could print and distribute them to the membership. This request was a bit forward

after Katherine just refused the ARCS position. The Red Cross executives quickly pa
lmed off this responsibility to Miss Fox.

Katherine provided a one month notice to the Central Council Nursing Education in Chicago. During the wait to leave, Katherine requested that the executives write a new Red Cross bulletin on nursing, which could be printed and distributed to the two million General Federation of Women's Clubs members. On January 11, 1921 she contacted Dr. Farrand of Red Cross, Washington, D.C. and requested that he contribute an article for the bulletin. In addition, Katherine requested that the Chairman of the Central Committee write portions of the proposed bulletin. On January 17, 1921 the Chairman responds, "I am overwhelmed with obligations of every sort. It will be quite impossible for me to do anything myself but I am sending your letter to Miss Fox." Miss Fox received the outline and responded, in part, "If you are able to get the proposed individuals to write for you, the article may be too long, too technical and too expensive to print two million copies." Dr. Farrand notified Katherine that he would not be able to write an article and also referred it to Miss Fox. Miss Fox composed three pages for this article, copy filed in Katherine's service file.[19]

"On February 8, 1921 there was a cable stating Olmsted is sailing to London on February 19th.[20] Unfortunately, the incidents continued while Katherine anticipated sailing to her new position abroad.

FIFTH INCIDENT – ATTITUDE AND OVERSTEPPING

Just before Katherine set sail for London and her new position as Director for League of Red Cross Societies, some altercation occurred. Miss Hays and Miss Noyes believed Katherine displayed an unacceptable attitude and overstepped her span of control. There are no specifics of the incident in her file, only extracts from letters alluding to Katherine's attitude.

On February 10, 1921, extracted from a letter to Miss Noyes, Washington, D.C. from Miss Hay, Europe, **"I can scarcely reconcile Miss Olmsted's attitude as reported by the Division Director** with her first acceptance of the position in this bureau."[21]

On March 1, 1921 – Answer by Miss Noyes: I am rather inclined to believe that Miss Olmsted's attitude is correct, for shortly after my arrival, I met Miss Lent who is her aunt, and the first statement she made was – "Well , of course, she would be in an independent position, in charge of the Public Health Work." I replied – had she had gone under our auspices instead of the League, she would have been assigned as your (Miss Hay's) assistant, responsible for the development of public health work – so I am inclined to believe that the situation has turned out satisfactorily all around." See letter filed 630.Europe, March 1, 1921.[22]

The Red Cross did not paper every nurse's file with a minutia of small details or reported incidents. Fellow nurse's files, who Katherine served with during that era, included thorough documentation but did not contain reported incidents. The incidents are unique to Katherine's file.

SIXTH INCIDENT – DUNNING MISS AN'NOYE'D

"On March 28, 1921 Katherine wrote from Geneva, Switzerland to Miss Elizabeth Fox, ARC Director of Public Health Nursing, Washington DC and dunned Miss Noyes claiming that she did not like the London nursing course and mentioned that Miss Noyes dismissed two American nurses from the program. Katherine stated, "I do so want to have these students carry back with them a better idea of what American nurses are doing than some of them gained from the unfortunate contact which they have had with the two who were practically dismissed from the course." The two nurses referred to are Miss Ledyard and Miss Simon. In the same letter, she also requested Red Cross pamphlets for distribution."[23]

"Miss Noyes responded on April 28, 1921 in a letter to Katherine. "I am sorry that you are under the mistaken impression that our two nurses were dismissed from the course. Our decision to withdraw them from the course and finish their training outside of London was based upon the intolerable situation in which they were placed. **I think you are altogether wrong** in supposing that the International students received an unfortunate impression of American nurses from Miss Ledyard and Miss Simon. I am quite sure you will find that the reverse is true. Glad to know you are finding life in Geneva interesting **and hope that the huge job you have undertaken will not be too discouraging.**"[24] Katherine, openly vocal in her opinion, was in conflict with the American Red Cross (ARC) team. The tone of the letter from Miss Noyes sounded very annoyed. Apparently, Katherine was an independent thinker and controlling her is not something the Red Cross was successful at.

SEVENTH INCIDENT – HEADSTRONG AND OVERLY VOCAL

There is not much detail regarding the seventh incident in the Red Cross file. Miss Ledyard was mentioned negatively in Katherine's correspondence previously, where she labeled her as an unfortunate contact at the London nursing school. Perhaps Miss Ledyard was stirring the pot of discontent? If so, the discontent burned lengthy for Miss Ledyard over ten months. The following incident is a file note, rather than copies of the actual letters.

January 4, 1922 entry in Katherine's Red Cross service file regarding her visit to Poland and her "going outside her right in advising and controlling". Miss Hays wrote that "it is unfortunate that Miss Ledyard appeared to have the exaggerated idea of the scope of Miss Olmsted's visit." In a reply to Miss Hays on January 26, 1922 Miss Noyes stated, "**I hope that all will continue to go well, although I have not much faith in that direction.**"[25]

Although Miss Hays defended Katherine, she also was not overly pleased with Katherine's attitude. On January 26, 1922 Miss Hays noted the following in a letter to Katherine, "With your unwillingness to admit any blame in this matter there is little use to prolong this discussion. Your first interoffice letter regarding your opinion of various phases of ARC nursing activities is referred to again because of **the spirit of its contents.**"[26]

And so it seemed that Miss Noyes was irritated with Katherine's behavior and Miss Ledyard may have reported inflated incidents about Katherine to get back at her, and Katherine's attitude was questionable. And yes, this was a whole bunch of drama.

EIGHTH INCIDENT – STATEMENT MADE IN LORCS BULLETIN

On February 23, 1922, Katherine published a statement in the LORCS Bulletin which was considered derogatory toward ARC. The example was not included in Katherine's service file, only a typed note regarding the incident. Dr. Hill recommended that Col. Bicknell should be consulted regarding the statement that Katherine had made in the bulletin. Col. Bicknell responded to Miss Hay, "**I am in entire sympathy with Miss Noyes' feeling but the incident is past** and the discussion which I have had with Sir Claude Hill re Miss Olmsted's tour will probably preclude a repetition of any similar occurrences." Letter filed 630.Europe.

On March 14, 1922 a letter from Miss Hay to Miss Noyes stated, "Miss Olmsted was in the office Saturday on route from London to Geneva. I purposely avoided any reference to our recent disagreements. With what I wrote to her directly and what Col. Bicknell has discussed with Sir Claude Hill, I believe there has been enough said for the present."[27]

After this incident, there is a void of documents in Katherine's American Red Cross Service file for the next three and a half years. No correspondence, notes, annual surveys, nothing, until notice of her return for a furlough in 1925. Katherine's 630.Europe file, as mentioned previously, with LORCS was most likely used during her three and a half years of service overseas. The 630.Europe file is not located on the National Archives website. In a letter dated March 3, 1922, Miss Noyes stated, "We have no information on Katherine Olmsted's travel plans, she is with the League of Red Cross Societies, not the American Red Cross. May I recommend another Red Cross nurse to speak at your function?"[28] This statement confirmed ARC's complete cutoff from Katherine and LORCS and perhaps the reason there is no documentation in their service file.

Based on an examination of Katherine's ARC Service File, eight incidents are observed over a three and a half year time span from 11/29/1918 to 3/14/1922. It is not known if any further incidents continued after her first year as Director of Public Health Nursing for LORCS. However, the years following Katherine's escape from the siege of Romania through her first year as Director in Europe were documented as turbulent times with the American Red Cross.

II

Europe League of Red Cross Societies

The League of Red Cross Societies was a new organization formed after World War I ended, when the American Red Cross began to withdraw from overseas. The book written by Henry P. Davison, Chairman of the War Council of the American Red Cross provides a good discussion of LORCS purpose.

> The Red Cross War Council, after consultation with the heads of its European commissions, instituted a cutting-down of production and a gradual diminishing of Red Cross work in the actual war areas, and an appreciable reduction in personnel everywhere. The Red Cross was to become as it was before the war, with the Executive Committee directing the American Red Cross.
>
> The League of Red Cross Societies was then adopted unanimously to prevent human suffering and to arouse all peoples to a sense of their responsibility for the welfare of their fellow beings throughout the world. Through its headquarters at Geneva, the League of Red Cross Societies planned to stimulate

peace-time activities of all National Red Cross Societies, and to help them grow and carry out a world-wide public health campaign. The National Red Cross Societies of each country would have the responsibility of the actual work of safeguarding and improving public health, but that each society should stimulate and encourage the natural agencies for such work within their respective countries, including the departments of health of their governments' and in cases where such departments do not exist, the societies should endeavor to create public sentiment for the establishment of such departments.

The League of Red Cross Societies was formed to supplement the work of the International Committee of the Red Cross of Geneva, acting in harmony with it. The League was in no way to supersede, absorb or conflict with the activities of the national societies. The League was to put at the disposal of the national societies the latest knowledge and approved practices of experts in public health and preventive medicines throughout the world.[1]

In brief, the League of Red Cross Societies was to help National Red Cross Societies of each country become organized, grow and take on public health challenges. The League of Red Cross Societies was not to perform the work, but to create public interest in establishing departments of health and local Red Cross Societies for their own countries. The American Red Cross Society would no longer be present overseas.

Alice Fitzgerald, Johns Hopkins class of 1906, remained in Europe after the war as Chief Nurse of the American Red Cross Commission in Europe starting in May 1919. She oversaw the demobilization all of the American Red Cross nurses still serving in Europe. In October 1919, she became the first Director of the Nursing Bureau of the League of Red Cross Societies in Geneva. She organized local nursing schools and public health nursing services according to American nursing standards in

Poland, Czechoslovakia, Romania, Hungary, Yugoslavia, Montenegro and Albania. She started the International School for Public Health Nurses for the Florence Nightingale International Foundation in London. Katherine Olmsted continued the work by organizing the second course at Bedford College at the University of London for public health nurses from all over the world. As the second Director of the Nursing Bureau of the League of Red Cross Societies, Katherine Olmsted also organized public health nursing services in Norway, Estonia and Latvia countries as well as continued those in the above listed countries.[2]

Katherine performed some very important work in Europe, as a Director for League of Red Cross Societies. She surveyed public health conditions, recruited nurses and developed nursing training programs. Europe is a conglomeration of many small countries, each about the size of a state in the U.S. in land mass, bunched together on the continent of Europe. During her second tour of duty in Europe, Katherine visited many countries to establish nursing agencies. Here are some different extracts that describe the work she performed.

In 1921 Katherine M. Olmsted accepted the position of Director of the Nursing Division of the League of Red Cross Societies- this League founded in 1919 by the Red Cross Societies of Great Britain, France, Italy, Japan and the United States on the initiative of Henry P. Davison, Chairman of the American Red Cross Council during the European war-its aim: "To promote Red Cross principles and activities throughout the world in time of peace." and her work was to organize a Red Cross service for nurses and establish training schools in every country in Europe.[3]

As Director it was Katherine's duty to assist in the establishment of Red Cross nursing schools and to recruit young women suitable for such training. With an office in Paris and an office in Geneva, she traveled to fifty-two countries. The young women selected were enrolled in the London nursing course she had established at Bedford College, the University of London and afterwards returned to their respective countries to organize nursing service. Katherine directed two international courses for women in Bedford College, London; 1) Public Health Nursing Course and 2) Hospital Administration Course.[4]

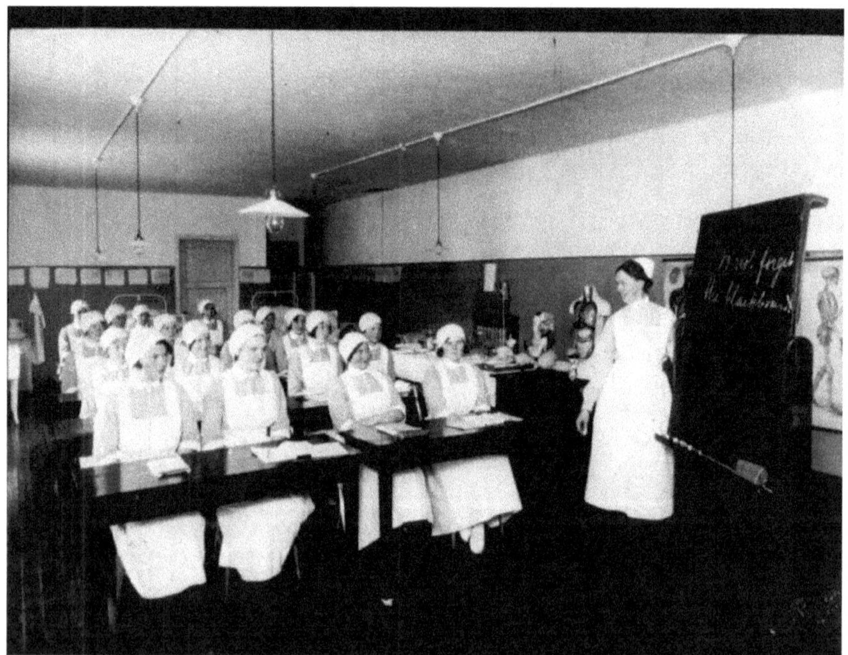

International Nursing Courses at Bedford College, London circa 1920s run by Leaguae of Red Cross Societies
IFCR/Editions de la Photscopie, Paris, Nursing archive, Bedford London, film strip number 40988

"The picture shows a classroom and students attending the international nursing courses held at Bedford College, College of Nursing in London. These courses were run by Katherine Olmsted and the League of Red Cross Societies. They were later taken over by the Florence Nightingale International Foundation."[5]

"Ever the pioneer, Katherine Olmsted was one of those instrumental in setting up the international nursing course at Bedford College, London, to provide opportunities for advanced work in nursing not available elsewhere, except the United States. The establishment of these courses was a milestone in nursing history. Nurses from all over the world enrolled, providing an inestimable influence upon the profession."[6]

The scope of the work that Katherine achieved was impressive during her second appointment in Europe. Other countries did not have nurse training schools or programs and Katherine finished work to develop nurse training classes. What a huge task to coordinate so many parts, spread out over a continent. And then consider a large part of this position was field work, assessing resources and locating potential nurse trainees. Based on Katherine's resume; "Many of these countries awarded Katherine decorations and citations for the work she performed."[7]

Katherine's travel to fifty-two countries is also impressive. This is a unique experience not many individuals have had in their lifetime. The exposure to so many different cultures and people would certainly provide an expanded viewpoint of the world. Specific stories and experiences Katherine had in a few of the countries are provided in the next few chapters.

12

Europe a Second Time

ROUMANIA

It seemed fitting that Katherine's first assignment in Europe was Romania with Queen Marie and the Royal Family. Romania was Katherine's service location during World War I and she had become acquainted with Queen Marie during that time. Perhaps Katherine chose Romania first, as her position was largely hers to create within the League's guidelines. Romania was a fine starting point, the area known to her and people she was familiar with. This excerpt tells of Katherine's first assignment, landing in Bucharest, the capital of Romania.

As Director, Katherine's first assignment was a return to Roumania. When she stepped off the train at Bucharest she was met by a typical Roumanian officer with a fierce waxed mustache and a red lined cape, who escorted her to Queen Marie's palace-really a simple white house set among trees. Here beautiful Queen Marie greeted her at the door, and honored her guest by wearing the Red Cross uniform. Katherine was given a suite with bedroom, sitting room and bath and she admits that she promptly used all the Royal stationery on the desk to write to her friends at home.

It was a cozy family scene on that first evening. King Ferdinand, with his feet on a chair, read a newspaper and Prince Carol, looked like an English school boy while he smoked a pipe. The Queen's daughters, the Queen of Greece, the Queen of Serbia and the Crown Princess Ileana joined them for dinner, signaled by trumpet and served on a large mahogany table set with gold plates.

Queen Marie and Katherine drove through Roumania every day to seek out prospective nurses for the weeks while she was their guest. One evening, Katherine attended the opera with the Royal Family. The audience waited outside the opera house and no one entered until Queen Marie drove up in her car and the red carpet was rolled out. The Queen stood in her Royal box as the audience entered. Not a soul sat down until, at the sound of a bell, their adored Queen blessed them with outstretched arms, followed by the strains of the Roumanian national anthem. Once the Queen was seated, everyone in the opera house sat down and the opera began.

As a thank you for the relief work, the Queen presented Katherine with a special decoration. It was a handsome medal issued at the time of her marriage to King Ferdinand, bearing their portraits-one of only three struck off. The second medal was in the possession of Queen Mary of England. Even more precious to Katherine, however, was the little iron cross she had received from the Queen after their work in the makeshift monastery hospital three and a half years earlier.[1]

Coronation Medal of Ferdinand I of Romania, presented to Katherine Olmsted by Queen Marie

Coronation Medal
Johns Hopkins University, Sheridan Libraries and Museums

Coronation medal back
Johns Hopkins University, Sheridan Libraries and Museums

Queen Marie presented Katherine Olmsted this circular bronze medal with two portraits and inscription "Ferdinand Regele Romaniei si Maria Regina" on front; reverse features a scene of soldiers on horseback by C. Kristescu with inscription "Inaiul rege al tuturor Romanilor incoronatu sa La Alba Julia in 15 X 1922" (The first king of all Romanians enthroned at La Alba on the 15th of October 1922).[2]

According to Anna Olmsted, the Romanian decoration is the first medal Katherine received as Director of Nursing for LORCS. Queen Marie and Katherine spent some weeks together driving through Romania to locate potential nursing candidates. With Katherine's second visit to Romania completed, there were many other countries on the list to visit.

BELGIUM

Belgium is nestled between France on the West and Germany to the East. The Netherlands are located to the north of Belgium and Luxembourg to the southeast. Brussels is the capital of Belgium. "Belgium is split between Dutch and Flemish speaking Flemings in the north, and French speaking Walloons in the south. The Ardennes region in southeast Belgium is well known for its beautiful natural scenery. Groves of walnut trees hide slate-roofed villages and remote castles."[3]

Katherine visited Belgium to locate recruits and establish training schools for nurses. "Countess Cecile Mechelynch, Director of the Nursing School in Brussels Belgium, later wrote to Katherine's cousin, Anna Olmsted, and recounted her experience. "I admired her character, energy and variety of interests. She has done much in Europe for nursing after World War I and I remember so well her lectures-so inspiring-she gave to us at the first International Course organized by the League of Red Cross Societies in London."[4]

Katherine received a humanitarian award from King Albert I for her work in Belgium. Surprisingly another individual, very well known, also received a humanitarian award at that ceremony.

Toward the end of her stay in Belgium, Katherine was honored at a garden party given by King Albert I in Brussels. She was summoned, together with Herbert Hoover, to approach the King. And the King presented to each of them a bronze medal with the engraved portraits of Edith Cavell and Marie de Page, President of the Belgian Red Cross, who had lost her life on the Lusitania. Katherine had worked with Hoover and recalled sitting with him in a conference in Paris along with participants from France, Italy and Germany. Katherine heard Hoover answer the arguments of each participant in his native language.[5]

Little did Katherine know that she was standing next to the man who would become the 31st President of the United States!

Herbert Clark Hoover was an American politician who served as the 31st president of the United States from 1929 to 1933.

World War I came to an end in November 1918, but Europe continued to face a critical food situation; Hoover estimated that as many as 400 million people faced the possibility of starvation. The United States Food Administration became the American Relief Administration (ARA), and Hoover was charged with providing food to Central and Eastern Europe. In addition to providing relief, the ARA rebuilt infrastructure in an effort to rejuvenate the economy of Europe. Throughout the Paris Peace Conference, Hoover served as a close adviser to President Wilson, and he largely shared Wilson's goals of establishing the League of Nations, settling borders on the basis of self-determination, and refraining from inflicting a harsh punishment on the defeated Central Powers. After U.S. government funding for the ARA expired in mid-1919, Hoover transformed the ARA into a private organization, raising millions of dollars from private donors. He also established the European Children's Fund, which provided relief to fifteen million children across fourteen countries.

The Russian famine of 1921–22 claimed six million people, but the intervention of the ARA likely saved millions of lives. When asked if he was not helping Bolshevism by providing relief, Hoover stated, "twenty million people are starving. Whatever their politics, they shall be fed! Reflecting the gratitude of many Europeans, in July 1922, Soviet author Maxim Gorky told Hoover that "your help will enter history as a unique, gigantic achievement, worthy of the greatest glory, which will long remain in the memory of millions of Russians whom you have saved from death".

In 1919, Hoover established the Hoover War Collection at Stanford University. He donated all the files of the Commission for Relief in Belgium, the U.S. Food Administration, and the American Relief Administration, and pledged $50,000 as an endowment (equivalent to $781,478 in 2021). Scholars were sent to Europe to collect pamphlets, society publications, government documents, newspapers, posters, proclamations, and other ephemeral materials related to the war and the revolutions that followed it. The collection was renamed the Hoover War Library in 1922 and is now known as the Hoover Institution Library and Archives.[6]

Kyle Perkins, Materials Analyst at the Herbert Hoover Presidential Library in Iowa, affirmed the validity of the Belgium award. The Library does indeed have this specific medal in the collection and Mr. Perkins provided some information regarding how it was made and provided a picture of front and back.

The medals, awarded to both Herbert Hoover and Katherine Olmsted, were designed by Belgian medalist and sculptor Armand Bonnetain and they were pressed and engraved in October 1919 by Fonson & Sons in Brussels. This medal is currently not on display in the Herbert Hoover Presidential Library, however is stored and catalogued. The printed reference for these medals is a book published in 1923 by Charles Lefebure. The medal held in the Library is an original 6cm, October 1919 bronze, with Edith Cavell and Marie de Page, President of the Belgian Red Cross engraved on the front and the inscription, on the reverse in English says, "1915 REMEMBER!"[7]

Katherine Olmsted's Bronze Medal of Edith Cavell and Marie de
Page, President of the Belgian Red Cross presented to her by King
Albert I, Brussels

Edith Cavell and Marie DePage medal front
Herbert Hoover Presidential Library and Museum

Edith Cavell was a British nurse working in German
occupied Belgium who was executed in 1915 by the Germans for
helping 200 Allied soldiers escape. Marie Depage was a Belgian
nurse, and wife of Dr. Amtoine Depage. She was killed on May
7, 1915 in the sinking of the RMS Lusitania. The Commission
De L'Ecole belge d'infirmieres diplomees, the nursing school
founded by Dr. Depage, issued this circular bronze medal in
1919, designed by Armand Bonnetain, manufactured by Fonson and Sons of Belgum. Medal features jugate busts of Edith
Cavell and Marie Depage in nursing uniforms facing the left
with an arching olive branch behind their heads on the right
side of the image; raised lettering around the rim on the front;
raised lettering on a plain reverse. Inscriptions Front: "MARIE
DEPAGE/EDITH CAVILL." Back "1915 REMEMBER!"[8]

CZECHOSLOVAKIA

"Prague, the capital of Czechoslovakia, is located approximately 842 miles NW of Bucharest. This area is mountainous and the city of Prague was a major European cultural center in medieval times. Much of the beautiful architecture remains, and old palaces house government institutions and academies of music and art."[9]

There are three references to Katherine's work in Czechoslovakia during her time as Director of Nursing Services. The first summary tells of Katherine's travel across the country with the President's children to recruit nurses. The second reference briefly mentioned Katherine training nurses and the third, a citation and thank you from the nurses of Czechoslovakia.

> Katherine received an urgent invitation to recruit nurses in Czechoslovakia. While in Prague, she was a guest in the Masaryk castle for six weeks. Jan Masaryk, the son of President Thomas Masaryk, drove her with his sister across Czechoslovakia in search of nurse recruits-especially proud of a new car which had been presented to him by an American officer. Part of the Masaryk castle was left in its medieval state, open to the public on certain days of the week. The other section with comfortable living quarters for the family had been modernized.

> Jan Masaryk, like his father, was immensely popular, a humanitarian with a virile personality and love of life. When in 1948 news of his death-an alleged suicide-was received, Katherine declared that he could not possibly have committed suicide. And information from his close friends made it clear that in order to cover up a Communist murder the false suicide report had been issued.[10]

A reference to Katherine's work performed is listed on her resume located at the National Archives. "While on the mission in Czechoslovakia, Katherine trained women for relief work under Lady Muriel

Paget."[11] "Lady Muriel Paget was a British philanthropist and humanitarian relief worker, initially based in London, and later in Central Europe. Lady Paget's work consisted of creating access to free kitchens, free medical aid and free clothing. She also inaugurated a system of traveling clinics for the benefit of those living in remote areas. Lady Paget received awards in recognition of her humanitarian work from Czechoslovakia and several other countries."[12]

In a thank you citation from the nurses of Czechoslovakia to Miss Olmsted– "May we tell you how appreciative we are of your position with the League of Red Cross Societies, so inspiring for all those who had the privilege to study under your kind leadership, to have attended your International Course in London, organized so carefully and imbued by the spirit of humanity, stimulating in us the ideals of the Lady of the Lamp."[13]

Katherine's work routine appeared to be similar in each country; she located nurse recruits and provided training. The thank you citation from the nurses she trained in Czechoslovakia sounded grateful and heartfelt.

LATVIA

"For her work in Latvia, Katherine Olmsted received a Latvian decoration never before given to a woman."[25]

> "We the Latvian nurses wish to express to you our heartfelt thanks and appreciation for the love and deep interest you have shown us and to the work. It is you who have who have furthered to such a great extent the development of nursing standards. You have inspired and encouraged us in our work, you have rendered us training and material assistance to our activities. Dear Miss Olmsted, we shall never forget you, we trust that also in your further work you will remember us in your heart, and we believe that the high ideals of our profession and cause we are working for will always be a tie between us."[26]

ESTONIA

Katherine Olmsted's Estonian Badge of the Red Cross Order

Estonia medal front
Johns Hopkins University, Sheridan Libraries and
Museums

The Estonian medal is a Greek cross made of gilt metal with white enamel border and red enamel filling; rays of 'light' burst from the center of the cross outward between the arms; in the center is a circle with scalloped edges with light blue enamel border, dark blue enamel stripe just inside the border, and a white enamel edge around a red enamel circle in the center of the cross with the letter "E". Reverse features a red enamel circle in the center of the cross with gold lettering; at the top of the cross is a white enamel lighthouse with metal rays of 'light' emanating from its beacon; suspended from a blue ribbon with white and navy blue stripes. Inscription Back; "INTER ARMA CARITA/1919" (Translataes:"Arms and Charity")[14]

Estonia medal back
Johns Hopkins University, Sheridan Libraries and Museums

FINLAND & BALTIC COUNTRIES SOUTH

The lengthiest description in Anna Olmsted's booklet is on Finland, which may have been due to the fact that Katherine spent quite some time in Finland and then nine weeks traveling with Baroness Sophia Mannerheim, according to her cousin, Anna Olmsted. Katherine specifically mentioned Baroness Sophia Mannerheim in written correspondence to the European Council for Nursing Education. In part it stated that "the Baroness Mannerheim and Miss Olmsted had made a considerable study of the work done by the Nursing Division and proposed an outline to promote nursing standards in Europe."[15] These two women found commonality in their work together.

Katherine's Finnish mission included a request for advice in establishing a training school for nurses at the University of Helsingfors where she was the guest of Baron Carl Mannerheim, Finland's national hero, and his sister Baroness Sophia Mannerheim. The Baroness had taken a nursing course in England and the two women worked on plans for the new school day after day—this of course in addition to journeying throughout the countryside on the usual nurse quest. At first they drove with shaggy Siberian ponies, later with a Buick, one of the first American cars to appear in Helsingfors, and like Masaryk's car, a present to the Baron from American officers. And Katherine taught him how to drive it!

Barron Mannerheim, a widower, was deeply disappointed in his two beautiful daughters. One, in spite of parental disapproval, was a professional dancer and had joined the Russian Ballet. The other, also against his wishes, had entered one of the strictest covenants in Europe, where nuns were never allowed to speak. During a special excursion Katherine accompanied the Baroness on a visit to the convent. The girl was allowed to talk to her aunt, but after years of silence she could scarcely speak.

In the evenings after strenuous days, Katherine was taken to the opera and the theatre and was also given a reception in her honor. "The Baron was exceedingly handsome," said Katherine, "and the Baroness was a stately beauty. The castle looked more like a jail on the outside, with gloomy stone walls and barred windows; the interior was very luxurious, with great fireplaces and superb furnishings."

For nearly nine weeks Katherine traveled with the Baroness, who knew innumerable languages and served as interpreter in Bulgaria, Greece, Yugoslavia and Albania; also known as the Baltic countries, as well as in Finland and Turkey. Heartbreaking conditions were found everywhere. Lithuania was miserable, devastated by typhus and over-run by the Bolsheviks; in Latvia only half the children had parents, the others were in orphanages; Austria and Hungary were suffering intensely. In Hungary, when she gave a doctor a medical magazine to which he had formerly subscribed, she was told that its subscription cost more than he could earn in a year!"[16]

"Finland is far to the north and about 24 hours travel from Romania, the top of the Baltic countries."[17] Turkey is located just south of Yugoslavia, the southernmost Baltic country. Baroness Sophia Mannerheim displayed true commitment to nursing when she accompanied Katherine on the extensive journey south to survey conditions. Based on the description, it does not appear that there were many women to recruit for nursing school in the Baltic countries, due to the post war conditions. "Katherine's resume stated that she trained women for relief work and care of orphans in the Baltic countries."[18] She may have conducted on-location training to alleviate the immediate needs.

"Katherine's resume also states that while she was in Greece, she worked with a joint distribution committee under Henry Morgenthau in exchange of peoples."[19] "Henry Morgenthau Sr. was an American Ambassador to the Ottoman Empire during WWI. He was an activist against Greek genocide, the killing of Christian Ottoman Greeks during WWI and afterwards on the basis of religion and ethnicity."[20] For this segment of Katherine's work, the process not only included locating nurse recruits, but making plans for a training school for nurses, surveying war devastated countries and providing on-location training.

POLAND

Poland has the Baltic Sea to the north and neighbors clockwise from two o'clock; Lithuania, Belarus, Ukraine, Czechoslovakia and Germany. The capital is Warsaw. "Poland is primarily non-mountainous with a temperate climate, however winters can be extremely cold and ice often closes northern harbors along the Polish Baltic coast. People still wear traditional dress, especially in the rural areas. The strong, well made garments last for a long time and these costumes are worn for festivals and folkdances."[28]

Katherine gave many talks about her time spent in Europe, after World War I. In January 1944, she addressed the Seneca Chapter of the Daughters of the American Revolution at their monthly meeting. The members of this organization share a common bond in that they can trace their lineage from patriots of the American Revolution. Here is a light-hearted recap of her experience in Poland, reported by the Geneva Daily Times newspaper.

> Among the most fascinating incidents which the speaker related was her acquaintance with a Polish princess. Miss Olmsted had been sent to Poland to secure the Princess for Red Cross training in London. At the railroad station where Miss Olmsted expected to be met by "honest-to-goodness royalty, she was met by an unassuming but beautiful girl in calico perched atop a hay wagon. The girl identified herself as the Princess, and Miss Olmsted and the girl proceeded to jog along toward the home of the former.
>
> The home of the Princess was an old Gothic castle. Residing with her was her white-haired grandmother and two very old servants. The rest of the family had been killed during the war, Miss Olmsted later determined.
>
> The Princess did go to London, arriving with "The History of Music" as her sole piece of baggage. She was trained in the Red Cross school there and in the University of London, where she became renowned for her love of examinations. Where ever there was an examination, there, in the front row, would be the Princess from Poland. She later returned to her own country to train other girls in similar work.[29]

HUNGARY
Katherine Olmsted's Merit Cross of the Hungarian Red Cross

Hungary medal front
*Johns Hopkins University, Sheridan Libraries and
Museums*

Hungary medal back
*Johns Hopkins University, Sheridan Libraries and
Museums*

This Hungarian breast badge is made of metal, silver gilt, in the shape of a Maltese cross with green enamel arms and rays between the arms; superimposed bronze gilt shield with white enamel featuring a red enamel cross in the center and a crown on top; tapered vertical pin on the back with engraving, Inscription back: "CRUX RUBRA HUNGARICA 1922."[21] The translation is Hungarian Red Cross.

ITALY
"While in Italy, Katherine Olmsted received an Highest Order of Merit, which was an Italian gold medal."[23]

Katherine Olmsted's Italian Red Cross Medal
of Merit for Propaganda
Medaglia dei Benemeriti per la Propaganda

Italy medal front
Johns Hopkins University, Sheridan Libraries and
Museums

Italy medal back
Johns Hopkins University, Sheridan Libraries and
Museums

This Italian medal is a circular silver medal with bas-relief of a Red Cross nurse holding a steaming bowl with a Greek cross in the background on the front; reverse features a Greek cross at the top, raised inscription in the middle and engraved name at the bottom; suspended from a silver ring for attaching

to a ribbon (now missing). Inscription back: "CROCE ROSSA/
ITALIANA" in raised lettering, "M. OLMSTED" engraved.[24]

NORWAY

Katherine Olmsted's Norwegian Red Cross Badge of Honor
Norges Rode Kor's Hederstegn

Norway medal front
*Johns Hopkins University, Sheridan Libraries and
Museums*

This Norwegian medal is a white enamel Greek cross
with a smaller red enamel Greek cross inset on the front; reverse
features the Norwegian coat of arms inset in metal and filled
with light red enamel; suspended from a white ribbon with red
edges and blue edge stripes; attached at the suspension ring is a
green enamel laurel wreath.[27]

Norway medal back
Johns Hopkins University, Sheridan Libraries and
Museums

ICELAND

Katherine's visit to Iceland locale was reminiscent of her 1918 escape from the siege of Romania through Lapland, located 150 miles north of the Arctic Circle. Iceland is an Island Nation due north of the United Kingdom and shares similar latitude with Lapland. Apparently, Katherine traveled to Iceland after an Icelandic nurse visited London and lobbied for a Red Cross unit to be founded in her country. Here is the amusing tale as reported by the Geneva Daily Times in 1944.

An Icelandic nurse, resembling Greta Garbo so much that all coming in contact with her fell at her feet, had made a visit to London to plead for a Red Cross unit in her native land. Miss Olmsted agreed to go and told of her arrival in Iceland, and being dropped in a basket from the ship. This was not exactly her idea of fun, but Miss Olmsted accomplished the feat with little or no difficulty, only to be confronted with an amazing sight. The streets of the town she first entered were blazing with electric lights. The reason, she afterward found out, was that the government furnished the power, so the people took full advantage of the existing facilities." [22]

SERBIA

Katherine Olmsted's Badge of the Serbian Red Cross

Serbia medal front
Johns Hopkins University, Sheridan Libraries and
Museums

Katherine Olmsted's Serbian medal is a red shield-shaped medal with a vertical stripe down the center and a white circle with a red cross in it ass the center of the shield. There is a gold colored wreath around the bottom and sides of the white circle and small shield with sun on the horizon and a lion and griffin on it, three stars above the small shield. The medal is fastened with a screw attached to the back of the medal and a round plate with a threaded hole in it and two small handles on it.[30]

"Overall, Katherine Olmsted received eleven decorations plus citations from the European countries she assisted."[31] The nurses who trained under Katherine exalted her kindness and compassion. Katherine advocated for communities she served. It is easy to see that the public just loved her. As well as the honors and recognitions outlined previously, there are multiple public speaking requests stateside noted in her Red Cross Service file. Examples of these include "Anne Strong, Director of School of Public Health Nursing, Boston, MA 2/27/1922 requested Katherine to speak."[32], "Mabel H. Maescher, Ohio State Association of Graduate Nurses 12/14/1926 requested Katherine to speak at graduation"[33] and "Horace Morison, Boston Health League 2/28/1922, inquired whether Katherine was returning to U.S. and would like to offer Katherine a position as Director of Nurses for the Boston Health League."[34]

13

Furlough 1925-1926

After almost five years of service overseas, from February 1921 – December 1925, Katherine took a furlough and returned to Wallington, NY to spend Christmas with her family and enjoy an extended break. There is a dearth of documents in Katherine's American Red Cross Service file from March 1922 – January 1926. However, the local newspaper was an excellent source for reporting Katherine's whereabouts.

> In 1925 Katherine went on furlough to the U.S. for several months. Mrs. Emma Olmsted and her daughter, Miss Katherine Olmsted, the latter of whom has been at the head of the Red Cross organization work in Europe for the past four years, have arrived in America for a furlough and are in Wallington, as guests at the Lent homestead and of Mr. and Mrs. Harry H. Olmsted. Miss Mary Lent of New York will also spend the holidays at the family home in Wallington.[1]

The Record supplied another update about Katherine's plans a month and a half later,

Miss Katherine Olmsted is absent on a tour through the US before returning to Paris, headquarters for the International Red Cross. She is head of the nursing division of the international organization. Miss Olmsted will return to the family home at Wallington in the spring for another brief vacation before returning to Europe where her mother, Mrs. Emma Olmsted will accompany her.[2]

After several years, Katherine seemed to have made amends with Elizabeth Fox, ARC National Director for Public Health Nursing Services. "On January 11, 1926, there is a thank you note to Katherine from Miss Elizabeth Fox for a Christmas gift. It was followed by an invitation from Miss Fox to visit Washington, D.C. for a meeting of nurses and field workers in March 1926"[3]

Also during this time period, there was mention in "Katherine's Red Cross service file that she traveled to Washington, D.C. Red Cross National Headquarters for a few days in February 1926 and purchased a service badge. The entry also stated that Miss Olmsted served with the Humanitarian Commission 1917-1918."[4]

The American Red Cross Service medal is a circular bronze with a band of blue enamel around the rim and a circle of white enamel in the center. Attached over the white center is a red enamel cross, suspended from a navy blue ribbon. Inscriptions around the rim on the front read; "SERVICE-AMERICAN RED CROSS". Stamped on the back; "TIFFANY & Co., N.Y.BRONZE".[5]

American Red Cross Service Medal

American Red Cross Service Medal
Johns Hopkins University, Sheridan Libraries and
Museums

Once the public found out that Katherine would be in the United States, the speaking requests started to pour in. "Katherine informed Washington Head Quarters that she had 28 talks scheduled to various groups. She also planned to go to Toronto April 12-15, 1926 to attend the Canadian Red Cross Meeting and talk to the students."[6] "There are two speaking requests in Katherine's Red Cross file, anticipating if they are on the visit list and would like to have Miss Olmsted speak. There is also a request from the Red Cross to speak at a meeting of nurses and field workers."[7] The Sodus Record reported a talk given to the local PTA in April 9, 1926 just before Katherine's trip to Toronto.

Katherine Olmsted spoke to the Sodus PTA with 175 in attendance and outlined the Red Cross organization and growth of the International League, which started from the union of the Red Cross societies of America, Italy, France, Great Britain and Japan, had grown to include 54 countries, practically all the organizations except those of Soviet Russia, Persia, and Turkey. Twenty five countries have organized for this work since 1919.

Miss Olmsted stated that the League of Red Cross Societies sponsors four main lines of activity; Relief and Disaster, Junior Red Cross Work, Public Health Instruction and Public Health Nursing. Miss Olmsted is the head of Public Health Nursing for LORCS. Her training, personality and ability made her an ideal leader for this work.

Following this organization talk, Miss Olmsted spoke at some length of conditions abroad especially among the children. She stated that in some sections 80% of the children are orphans; that in many homes, all the houses will hold are being cared for by one house mother, who has found it in her heart to make a refuge for the children of "her sister, her neighbors, and those who came down the road." Wandering in from just anywhere, seeking food and shelter.

A very appealing part of her address was that telling of the joy with which the children in the desolate lands receive the things sent them by the Junior Red Cross workers in America, who cannot realize the pleasure their contributions bring to the hungry hearted orphans.

Those hearing Miss Olmsted were made to feel how great the opportunity is in this field, and it is hoped that the seed sown will not fall on barren ground, but will spring up and bear fruit a thousand fold.

With one of our own people directly in charge of these opportunities, it seems as though Sodus should do much to help Miss Olmsted put over this relief work, which is as much our work as hers.[8]

After six months furlough and many speaking engagements, "Katherine and her mother returned to Paris with her Aunt Kathryn Lent joining them in May 1926."[9] The sailing journey from New York to Paris overseas generally took about a month in the 1900's.

14

Resignation

From March 10, 1926 until 1928, there is only one document, a resignation letter, filed in Katherine's Red Cross Service file. Unfortunately, Katherine's resignation letter is not dated, nor was it stamped with a received date. There are however, some clues of surrounding event dates.

- "After six months furlough, Katherine returned to Europe in May 1926."[1]
- "The Latvian nurses received notice that Katherine Olmsted was leaving her present position. After her resignation from the Red Cross, there followed several months of much needed rest in France, ending with a special course at the University of the Sorbonne in Paris."[2]
- "Le Cordon Bleu Cuisine Diploma has intake for applicants four times a year; January, April, July and October with duration of six months Intensive or nine months Standard."[3]
- "The Record reported Katherine's return to New York on February 25, 1927.[4]

An educated estimate is that Katherine's resignation was almost immediate upon her return to Europe, based on about one month to sail from New York to Paris and the surrounding date clues.

May 1926	Jun 1926	July 1926	Dec 1926	Jan 1927	Feb 1927
New York to Paris, FR	Arrive Paris & Resign	Attend U of Sorbonne	Graduate w/Cordon Bleu Diploma	Rest, accumulate décor items	Paris, FR to New York

In an emphatic resignation letter Katherine stated in part, "Baroness Mannerheim has definitely requested that the Nursing Division of the League act as headquarters for the International Council of Nurses. The governing board of the European Council disagrees, therefore, I tender my resignation and sever all connection with the European Council for Nursing Education."[5] The tone of the resignation letter sounded irate that the Council disagreed with Baroness Mannerheim and Katherine Olmsted's proposition. It is also clearly stated that Katherine was completely done with her position.

TO THE PRESIDENT
        EUROPEAN COUNCIL FOR NURSING EDUCATION.

Dear Madam:

        Inasmuch as the proposal of utilising the Secretariat
of the League of Red Cross Socities does not meet with the unani-
mous approval of the Governing Board of the European Council for
Nursing Education, it would seem unwise for the Nursing Division
of the League to undertake any further responsibility in connection with the Council.

        And, inasmuch, as Baroness Mannerheim has definitely
requested that the Nursing Division of the League undertake to
act as a headquarters for the International Council of Nurses in
a similar capacity as was offered to the European Council and has
after considerable study of the work being done by the Nursing
Division, expressed for the members of the Executive Board of the
International Council of Nursing their full approval and appreciation of the methods of promoting nursing standards and feel that
it would be greatly to their advantage to work in the future in
close co-operation with the League of Red Cross Socities. I
therefore, beg to tender my resignation and sever all connection
with the European Council for Nursing Education.

                        /s/ KATHERINE OLMSTED

                        Chief - Division of Nursing
                        League of Red Cross Socities.

        see orginal copy filed E.C.N.E.

As you may recall in the earlier chapter, Europe League of Red Cross Societies, the League's defined purpose was to help each country establish their own National Red Cross Society. The League was charged with helping each nation become organized, grow and take on their own public health challenges. The League of Red Cross Societies was not to perform the work. So herein lies the difference of opinion. The governing board of the European Council did not approve that the Nursing Division of the League become headquarters for the International Council of Nurses in Europe, perhaps because this would place LORCS as an integral part of the European work. On the other hand, Katherine may not have intended for the International Council of Nurses to become involved with daily operations.

This disappointing miscommunication appeared to have led up to Katherine's resignation. However, it was her resignation that led to an important change in career paths. Katherine's next career had a huge impact on her next community, which is another story in itself. Look for Miss Olmsted's Normandy Inn, which tells of Katherine's experiences stateside in the next book.

The League continued on with the European restoration work after Katherine's departure. Maynard Carter and his wife, Katherine's Successor, later came to visit and stay with Katherine in 1956. It was in Carter's reminiscence of this time with Katherine that he provided information in an article written for the Old Internationals Newsletter.

Mrs. Maynard Carter of England accepted the position of Director after Katherine resigned, she had been Katherine's Assistant Director. From Mrs. Maynard L. Carter in England: "As I ponder over the past thirty years and years I worked with Katherine Olmsted in London and Paris, I realize more and more the strength and value of the foundation for nursing laid by Katherine. I realize that I who succeeded her and Yvonne Hentsch who followed me, could do no more than build upon these foundations of which the corner stone had been so well laid.[6]

"The Old Internationals Association was created in 1925 by Mrs. Maynard Carter who stated in the American Journal of Nursing, it was Katherine Olmsted's earnest wish to unite all former students of the international courses in a living union."[7] At a later time, Yvonne Hentsch, the third Director of the Nursing Division of the League wrote a letter to Anna Olmsted, Katherine's cousin.

> Yvonne Hentsch, Director Nursing Bureau, League of Red Cross Societies, Geneva, Switzerland said of Katherine's service, In her capacity as Director of the Nursing Division she was instrumental in establishing standards and policies which are still followed today. Her signature appear on so many valuable documents in the early history of the Nursing Bureau of the league that it is in some way as if her inspiration and thought had stayed with us, her successors, ever since she left the League in 1926. The League therefore owes her a deep debt of gratitude.[8]

And a fellow Red Cross Nurse, Alta Dines, also wrote to Anna Olmsted and recalled early days spent with Katherine.

> Alta Dines, Chairman of the Nursing Committee of the National Red Cross wrote, One of Katherine's great contributions was her preeminent share in founding the International Nursing Course at Bedford College, University of London, which drew nurses from many countries. In this Katherine Olmsted played a key role, leading to the formation of the Florence Nightingale Foundation.[9]

Katherine had a great influence on international nursing and was well thought of by her peers, as summarized by her co-workers. According to her cousin, Anna Olmsted, "Christmas greetings from European countries came to her regularly for many years."[10] Katherine was well thought of by the nurses she trained according to the citations she received. And most importantly, how highly thought of she was by the various countries' leaders who awarded her many medals for her humanitarian work.

Just as one journey completes, another adventure awaits. Katherine had made plans for that next adventure and her story is still inspiring today, for anyone wishing for a new career path.

15

❦

A New Adventure

Once free of nursing responsibility, Katherine put into action her plan for a new career. "After resigning the Red Cross, in 1926, Katherine enrolled in the University of the Sorbonne Cordon Bleu cooking school in Paris, before leaving Europe."[1] She reinvented herself with a new purpose, to begin a new career adventure in life.

According to Anna Olmsted, Katherine's cousin, "the Cordon Bleu cooking course held at the University of the Sorbonne in Paris had a stiff schedule. Katherine watched demonstrations by master chefs and then practiced cooking from six a.m. until six p.m."[2] Based on Anna Olmsted's description, it seems likely that Katherine enrolled in the six month Intensive Program for the diploma, rather than the nine month Standard Program. The six month Intensive Program better fits into the estimated timeline, mentioned earlier and is a strong match for Katherine's energetic personality.

Sorbonne University, Paris early 1900s
Sorbonne-universite.fr

Le Cordon Bleu, Paris website describes the Cuisine Diploma as a comprehensive and rigorous training programme that allows the progressive learning of French culinary techniques. The programme is taught by Le Cordon Bleu Paris Chefs, who have worked in some of the world's finest restaurants. With the knowledge gained from a rigorous training, students who have completed the Diplome de cuisine will be ready for a career in a professional kitchen or embark on a career change in French cuisine. The course teaches French culinary techniques, classic dishes and regional French and European cuisines. The teaching method is comprised of demonstrations, practical classes and theory classes. Intake for applicants is four times a year; January, April, July and October with duration of 6 months Intensive or 9 months Standard.[3]

"The Record mentioned Katherine's return with her mother Emma and aunt Kathryn upon completion of the Cordon Bleu course on February 25, 1927 to New York City where they stayed with Mary Lent, her aunt and then they returned to Wallington on March 25, 1927."[4] "The Arms' Crossroads Wallington reported that Katherine returned from France with a young French chef named Fernand"[5]

And apparently, they brought a lot of stuff with them to decorate the new tea shop. The Syracuse Herald American reporter Van Wormer stated, "the freight bill upon reaching the U.S. was nearly $1,000 in 1927."[6] The Sodus Record local paper provided a description of items.

They arrived with a large collection of French copper, pewter, brass, colorful pottery, china, French Provincial furniture and tapestries. Katherine brought with her marvelous European antiques, largely gifts from Queen Marie as a token of her deep appreciation for Olmsted's work in Rumania during the war. Among the items was a large collection of brass and copper cooking utensils, and heavy Polish and Rumanian cookware. These items would provide the atmosphere that reminded her so much of that of Normandy in France.[7]

European brass and copper displayed at the
Normandy Inn
Sodus Historical Society

The change in careers from nursing to owning a tea shop is a vastly a different line of work. A nursing position reports to a hospital or organization versus a tea shop proprietor and no boss. The tasks of planning, cooking and serving meals as well as managing all business decisions is quite a divergence from training nurses and caring for ill people. However, "after Katherine's wartime experience in Romania and almost starving, where no meats, fats, butter or eggs were available;"8 perhaps owning a tea shop with plenty of food for everyone is not so difficult to understand. Hamilton B. Allen, a food critic from the Rochester area, mentioned in his column that he had been a customer of the Normandy Inn since the 1930s and his description of how Katherine founded the Normandy Inn also provided a clue as to why Katherine chose this career path.

> Hamilton B. Allen, a food critic from the Rochester area, stated that he had been a customer of the Normandy Inn since the 1930s. Allen said, "Katherine had become smitten with the charm of provincial France and the little family run dining rooms, which she discovered during post-Armistice travels. She decided to create a dining room which would recapture the charm and flavor of the French originals which inspired her, in her Lake Ontario homeland."9

Allen's brief quote described how Katherine brought what she was fond of in Europe to the United States and created a family-run style dining room. Her new career was focused on fun experiences and good food, things that were lacking from her very early experience in war torn Romania and perhaps some of the post WWI countries. The focus on entertainment and plenty of food certainly offered an opposite perspective of the lighter side of life.

The Sodus Record reported that "Katherine opened the "Auberge N'ormande" her Tea Shop in June 1927."10 "Katherine started her business venture in an old dry house on her Brother Harry's farm on Maxwell Creek. She then pursued her lifelong dream of bringing a little of Normandy, France to the United States."11 Auberge means hotel or inn in the French language. And so Auberge, N'ormande is the French pronunciation for Normandy Inn.

The mill on brother Harry Olmsted's farm, Katherine's first
Normandy Inn
*Arm's Crossroads Wallintong, The Wallington Cobblestone Schoolhouse Restoration
Committee*

During her ownership and management of the Normandy Inn, Katherine continued volunteer nursing service work stateside. She was a great asset to the community. According to her resume, written by her own hand, and housed in the National Archives:

- Case Supervisor of Wayne County, NY – Temporary Emergency Relief Association
- Chairman, Western District, State Federation of Home Bureau for 2 years and served on Federation Nutrition Committee and Education Committee
- Authorized teacher under Red Cross for Canteen, Nutrition and Home Nursing Classes
- Chairman, Wayne County, NY Red Cross Emergency Disaster and Relief Organization
- Minuteman, Civilian Protection
- State Program Director, Office of Civilian Mobilization, New York State War Council, Albany, New York
- New York State Nursing for War Service Executive Board[12]

Katherine Olmsted, circa 1935
Sodus Historical Society

Katherine's younger years included six years of college; three in art/ humanities and three in nursing school. The following years she served as a nurse were impactful to the communities, both on the home front and overseas. She progressed from student nurse to identifier of needs and teacher in the nursing field. Katherine's war time experience, as written by herself, displayed an amazing perspective from on-site war time deployment. After returning home, her exuberance and choice of actions clashed at times with the Red Cross executives, however her service to the community remained at the forefront of every choice. Katherine's ability to observe a situation and create a plan were impressive, as observed in her return to Europe for a second tour of duty, during reconstruction efforts post WWI. She traveled to fifty-two European countries; her mission was to recruit nurses and set up nurse training programs at each location. Katherine received eleven medals plus commendations from the heads of countries and the nurses she trained overseas.

After resigning, Katherine reinvented herself with new purpose, to begin a new adventure in life as restauranteur in the United States. Seen over and over again, Katherine had a hugely positive impact with every person she worked with. This trait continued on in her new line of work and flowed into an entire community.

If you loved this adventure of Miss Olmsted, you may look forward to *Miss Olmsted's Normandy Inn* book, previously released, which tells about the second half of Katherine's life. Find out how Katherine took on the small town of Wallington, NY, created jobs for families during the Great Depression when work was scarce, and endeared herself to the local community.

SOURCES

Aberg, Elsa. 1939. "The Old Internationals". *The American Journal of Nursing.* Vol. 39 No. 5 (May 1939) 480-482. https://www.jstor.org/stable/3413898

Bedford College picture *Ifrc.org.* The International Federation of Red Cross and Red Crescent Societies. https://shared.ifrc.org/record/165305/media_id/165544 (2023)

Carter, Maynard L. 1956. "With Katherine Olmsted in Normandy Inn as seen by an Old International". *Old International's News Letter.* (October, 1956) 20-23.

Cooper, Signe S. R.N. *Wisconsin Nursing Pioneers,* "Katherine Olmsted, Public Health Teacher", University Extension, the University of Wisconsin Department of Nursing (1968) 13-14.

Davison, Henry P. *The American Red Cross in the Great War.* New York: The Macmillan Company, 1920. Reprinted by Leopold Classic Library, North Haven, CT.

Dines, Alta Elizabeth, "In Memoriam, Katherine Olmsted-1912". *The Alumnae Magazine,* Volume 63, No 3. September 1964.

Exhibits: The Sheridan Libraries and Museums, Hopkins and the Great War. https://exhibits.library.jhu.edu/exhibits/show/hopkins-and-the-great-war/school-of-nursing/post-war-reconstruction/katherine-olmsted

"History & Mission". Jhu.edu. Johns Hopkins University. https://www.jhu.edu/about/history/ . (accessed 2023).

"Johns Hopkins Hospital, School for Nurses". Jhmi.edu. Medical Archives Catalog.https://medicalarchivescatalog.jhmi.edu/johnshopkinshospital/school-for-nurses/ . (accessed 2023).

"Katherine Olmsted of the Red Cross 1942". *The Syracuse Museum of Fine Arts: Quarterly Bulletin.* Volume 3, Number 2. Syracuse, N.Y. (Jan-Mar 1942) 7.

LaGorce, John Oliver, "Roumania and its Rubicon", *The National Geographic Magazine*, Washington, D.C. Vol. XXX, No. 3. (September 1916) 185-200.

Le Cordon Bleu, Paris "Cuisine Diploma-Paris". https://www.cordonbleu.edu/paris/cuisine-diploma/en (2023) searched (May 14, 2023).

"National Archives Catalog: American Red Cross Historical Nurse Files." 1978. *Collection ANRC: Records of the American National Red Cross,* February 12, 1978 https://catalog.archives.gov/search?page=1&q=katherine %20Olmsted.
Note- scanned file is mislabeled as Kathleen M. Olmstead, however contents clearly state Katherine M. Olmsted. Reported to National Archives June 11, 2023.

Olmsted, Anna Wetherill, *The Story of An American Red Cross Nurse,* Self-published pamphlet, circa 1967.

Readers Digest. *The Children's World Atlas.* London England: Ilex Publishers Ltd. "South East Europe." (1991).

Wadsworth, Eliot. 1917. "The Red Cross Spirit". *The National Geographic Magazine,* Volume XXXI, Number 5. (May 1917) 467.

Wallington Cobblestone Schoolhouse Restoration Committee. *Arms'Crossroads-Wallington.* Lyons, NY: Wilprint, Inc, 1982.

CITATIONS

CHAPTER1

1. Wallington, 68.
2. Ibid
3. National Archives, file 2 of 2, 66.
4. "Miss Mary Lent Dies At Wallington Home". *The Sodus Record*, Sodus, NY. Volume L, Number 32, November 14, 1946.
5. Wallington, 70.
6. National Archives, file 2 of 2, 49.
7. Johns Hopkins Nursing School, accessed September 27, 2023. https://medicalarchivescatalog.jhmi.edu/johnshopkinshospital/school-for-nurses/
8. Johns Hopkins University website accessed July 2023 https//www.jhu.edu
9. National Archives, file 2 of 2, 49.
10. Dines, 94.
11. National Archives, file 2 of 2, 49.

CHAPTER 2

1. Cooper, 14.
2. National Archives, file 1 of 2, 153.
3. National Archives, file 1 of 2, 151.
4. Wallington, 82.
5. National Archives, file 1 of 2, 131.
6. National Archives, file 2 of 22, 66.
7. Cooper, 13 – 14.
8. "Wisconsin Will Train its Community Nurses", *Ladysmith News-Budget*. Ladysmith, Wisconsin, May 12, 1916.
9. Olmsted, 1.
10. National Archives, file 1 of 2, 126-7.
11. National Archives, file 1 of 2, 124.
12. National Archives, file 1 of 2, 122.

13. National Archives, file 1 of 2, p.120.

14. National Archive, file 1 of 2, 106.

15. National Archives, file 1 of 2, 114-9.

16. Hopkins and the Great War Exhibit, accessed September 29, 2023. Post-war Reconstruction · Hopkins and the Great War · Exhibits: The Sheridan Libraries and Museums (jhu.edu)

CHAPTER 3

1. *World War I: The Great War*, Produced by Ten Worlds Entertainment, The History Channel Executive Producer Carl Lindahl. Disc 1 – Secrets of WWI. A & E Television Networks (2008), Blu-ray Disc, AAAE143940.

2. Wadsworth, 467.

3. Davison, 7-13.

4. "Anderson to Head Red Cross Unit - Third American Relief Commission to be Located in Rumania", *The Post Star*, Glens Falls, NY, August 14, 1917.

5. National Archives, file 1 of 2, 21-2.

CHAPTER 4

1. National Archives, file 1 of 2, 16.

2. Ibid

3. Olmsted, 2.

4. National Archives, file 1 of 2, 16.

5. Olmsted, 2-3.

6. National Archives, file 1 of 2, 16.

7. Davison, 235-6.

8. Olmsted, 2-3.

9. Ibid

10. Dictionary "Versts" accessed March 9, 2023 https://www.dictionary.com/browse/verst

11. Olmsted, 5.

12. Davison, 236.

CHAPTER 5

1. Olmsted, 5.

2. "Russian Freedom medal presented to Katherine Olmsted by Russian Premier Alexander Kerensky." *Exhibits: The Sheridan Libraries and Museums*, accessed September 27, 2023, https://exhibits.library.jhi.edu/items/show/560.

3. "Russian cross presented to Katherine Olmsted while on route to Roumania."

Exhibits: The Sheridan Libraries and Museums, accessed September 27, 2023, https://exhibits.library.jhi.edu/items/show/561.

4. Olmsted, 5.

5. Dictionary "Billet" accessed March 9, 2023 https://www.dictionary.com/browse/billet.

6. "Interesting Information from Miss Olmsted: Jassy, Roumania October 4th, 1917". *The Record,* Sodus, NY, January 19, 1918.

7. Encyclopedia Britannica, s.v. "Typhus" accessed May 25, 2023 https://www.britannica.com/science/typhus

8. "Interesting", *The Record,* Sodus, NY, January 19, 1918.

9. Ibid

10. Ibid

11. Davison, 237.

12. "Interesting Information from Miss Olmsted: Continued from last week October 10th, 1917". *The Record,* Sodus, NY, January 25, 1918.

13. Davison, 237.

14. "Interesting" *The Sodus Record,* January 25, 1918.

15. LaGorce, 186.

16. LaGorce, 188-190.

17. LaGorce, 195.

18. Davison, 238.

19. "Interesting" *The Sodus Record,* January 25, 1918.

20. Ibid

21. "Interesting Information from Miss Olmsted: Continued from last week October 14th, 1917".*The Record,* Sodus, NY, February 1, 1918.

22. Ibid

23. Olmsted, 6.

24. "Interesting", *The Sodus Record,* February 1, 1918.

25. Olmsted, 7.

26. "Another Letter From Miss Olmsted: Carried by William T. Ellis December 10, 1917", *The Sodus Record,* February 22, 1918.

27. Ibid

28. Davison, 246.

29. Olmsted, 7.

30. Davison, 247.

31. Davison, 248.

32. "Barbee Cross presented to Katherine Olmsted by Queen Marie of Romania." *Exhibits: The Sheridan Libraries and Museums,* accessed September 27, 2023, https://exhibits.library.jhi.edu/items/show/558.

CHAPTER 6

1. Olmsted, 6.
2. "Miss Olmsted Returns Home: Red Cross Nurse Makes Perilous Trip From Roumania to England: Ten Weeks on Train – Many Narrow Escapes", *The Sodus Record*, Volume XXII, Number 8. May 31, 1918.
3. New York Times, May 1918.
4. Georgia State Railroad Museum, Savannah, GA. Visited March 2023.
5. Olmsted, 9.
6. "Miss Olmsted", *The Sodus* Record, May 31, 1918.
7. Lynch, Grace. "Strange War Time Journey: The Way it Used To Be". *The Fulton Patriot*, June 6, 1968. Also Olmsted, 10.
8. Olmsted, 9.

CHAPTER 7

1. "Miss Olmsted", *The Sodus* Record, May 31, 1918.
2. Olmsted, 10.
3. "Miss Olmsted", *The Sodus* Record, May 31, 1918.
4. Ibid
5. Ibid
6. Ibid
7. Olmsted, 11.
8. Ibid
9. "Miss Olmsted", *The Sodus* Record, May 31, 1918.
10. "Great Lakes Vanished War Ships". *Expedition Unknow,* Discovery Channel, air date June 28, 2023.
11. "Miss Olmsted", *The Sodus* Record, May 31, 1918.
12. Olmsted, 11.

CHAPTER 8

1. "Miss Olmsted", *The Sodus* Record, May 31, 1918.
2. Ibid
3. National Archives, file 1 of 2, 125.
4. Google Maps, searched June 2023 "42 Grosvenor Place, London", https://www.google.com/maps/place/42+Grosvenor+Pl,+London.
5. National Archives, file 1 of 2, 18.

CHAPTER 9

1. "Miss Olmsted", *The Sodus* Record, May 31, 1918.

2. Ibid

3. National Archives, file 1 of 2, 103.

4. Olmsted, 13.

5. National Archives file 1 of 2, 101-7.

6. *The Lyons Republican*, June 14, 1918.

7. National Archive file 1 of 2, 83-100.

8. *The Sodus Record*, September 6, 1918.

9. National Archive file 1 of 2, 84.

10. National Archives file 2 of 2, 49.

11. National Archives file 1 of 2, 93.

12. National Archives file 1 of 2, 85.

13. *The Sodus Record*, October 18, 1918.

14. National Archives file 1 of 2, 83-4.

CHAPTER 10

1. National Archives file 1 of 2, 80 & 82.

2. National Archives file 1 of 2, 75.

3. National Archives file 1 of 2, 73-74.

4. Ibid

5. National Archives file 1 of 2, 70-71.

6. National Archives file 1 of 2, 63-64.

7. National Archives file 1 of 2, 61.

8. National Archives file 1 of 2, 60.

9. National Archives file 1 of 2, 47.

10. National Archives file 1 of 2, 21.

11. National Archives file 1 of 2, 40-45.

12. National Archives file 1 of 2, 40.

13. National Archives file 1 of 2, 39.

14. National Archives file 1 of 2, 44.

15. National Archives file 1 of 2, 33-35.

16. *Exhibits: The Sheridan Libraries and Museums*, accessed September 27, 2023 https://exhibits.library.jhu.edu/exhibits/show/hopkins-and-the-great-war/school-of-nursing/post-war-reconstruction/katherine-olmsted

17. National Archives file 1 of 2, 33.

18. "Miss Olmsted Returns Home: Red Cross Nurse Makes Perilous Trip From Roumania to England: Ten Weeks on Train – Many Narrow Escapes". *The Record* Sodus, NY, Volume XXII, Number 8, May 31, 1918.

19. National Archives file 1 of 2, 13-4 & 21-24.

20. National Archives file 2 of 2, 129.

21. National Archives file 2 of 2, 112.

22. Ibid

23. National Archives file 2 of 2, 126.

24. National Archives file 2 of 2, 121.

25. National Archives file 2 of 2, 113.

26. National Archives file 2 of 2, 115.

27. National Archives file 2 of 2, 106.

28. National Archives file 2 of 2, 107.

CHAPTER 11

1. Davison, 281, 285-6

2. *Exhibits: The Sheridan Libraries and Museums,* accessed September 27, 2023. Alice Fitzgerald · Hopkins and the Great War · Exhibits: The Sheridan Libraries and Museums (jhu.edu)

3. "Miss Olmsted will address DAR meeting, Seneca Chapter", *Geneva Daily Times,* January 17, 1944.

4. National Archives file 2 of 2, 49.

5. org, searched Florence Nightingale, August 2023.

6. Cooper, 14.

7. National Archives file 2 of 2, 50.

CHAPTER 12

1. Olmsted, 13-14.

2. "Coronation Medal of Ferdinand I of Romania, presented to Katherine Olmsted by Queen Marie." *Exhibits: The Sheridan Libraries and Museums,* accessed September 27, 2023, https://exhibits.library.jhi.edu/items/show/559.

3. Reader's Digest, 66.

4. Olmsted, 18.

5. Olmsted, 17.

6. Perkins, Kyle 2023. MA, Herbert Hoover Presidential Library and Museum. West Branch, IA. Correspondence with Pamela Lee. April 13, 2023.

7. Ibid

8. Armand Bonnetain, "Katherine Olmsted's Marie Depage and Edith Cavell medal." Manufactured by Fonson and Sons of Belgium. *Herbert Hoover Presidential Library,* and verified by Anna W. Olmsted's private collection photograph 1965, prior to donating all Katherine Olmsted's medals to Johns Hopkins Alumnae Association.

9. Reader's Digest, 78.

10. Olmsted, 14.

11. National Archives file 2 of 2, 50.

12. https://www.encyclopedia.com/women/dictionaries-thesauruses-pictures-and-press-releases/paget-muriel-1876-1938

13. "Katherine Olmsted of the Red Cross 1942". *The Syracuse Museum of Fine Arts: Quarterly Bulletin.* 7.

14. "Katherine Olmsted's Estonian Badge of the Red Cross Order." *Exhibits: The Sheridan Libraries and Museums,* accessed September 27, 2023, https://exhibits.library.jhi.edu/items/show/565.

15. National Archives file 2 of 2, 103.

16. Olmsted, p.15.

17. https://www.google.com/maps/dir/Romania/Finland

18. National Archives file 2 of 2, 50.

19.

20. https://www.britannica.com/biography/Hans-Morgenthau, accessed September 2023

21. "Katherine Olmsted's Merit Cross of the Hungarian Red Cross." *Exhibits: The Sheridan Libraries and Museums,* accessed September 27, 2023, https://exhibits.library.jhi.edu/items/show/562.

22. *Geneva Daily Times,* January 22, 1944.

23. "Miss Olmsted will address DAR meeting, Seneca Chapter", *Geneva Daily Times,* January 17, 1944.

24. Tailetti, P., "Katherine Olmsted's Italian Red Cross Medal of Merit for Propaganda." *Exhibits: The Sheridan Libraries and Museums,* accessed September 27, 2023, https://exhibits.library.jhi.edu/items/show/566.

25. "Miss Olmsted will address DAR meeting, Seneca Chapter", *Geneva Daily Times,* January 17, 1944.

26. Ibid

27. "Katherine Olmsted of the Red Cross 1942". *The Syracuse Museum of Fine Arts: Quarterly Bulletin.* 7.

28. Tiffany and Company, New York. "Katherine Olmsted's Norwegian Red Cross Badge of Honor." *Exhibits: The Sheridan Libraries and Museums,* accessed September 27, 2023, https://exhibits.library.jhi.edu/items/show/568.

29. Readers Digest, 80.

30. Gassners & J. Vilgins Riga. "Katherine Olmsted's Badge of Serbian Red Cross." *Exhibits: The Sheridan Libraries and Museums,* accessed September 27, 2023, https://exhibits.library.jhi.edu/items/show/567.

31. "Miss Olmsted will Address DAR Meeting, Seneca Chapter", *Geneva Daily Times,* January 22, 1944.

32. National Archives file 2 of 2, 50.

33. National Archives file 2 of 2, 108.

34. National Archives, file 2 of 2, 99.

CHAPTER 13

1. *Sodus Record*, December 25, 1925.
2. *Sodus Record*, February 12, 1926.
3. National Archives file 2 of 2, 84-5 & 95.
4. National Archives file 2 of 2, 88.
5. Johns Hopkins, Sheridan Libraries & University Museums. "Hopkins and the Great War Exhibit; Katherine Olmsted." *Exhibits: The Sheridan Libraries and Museums.*
6. National Archives file 2 of 2, 84-5.
7. National Archives file 2 of 2, 90 & 99.
8. "Miss Olmsted Tells Appealing Story", *Sodus Record*, April 9, 1926.
9. *Sodus Record*, May 1926.

CHAPTER 14

1. *Sodus Record*, March 19, 1926.
2. Olmsted, 17.
3. Le Cordon Bleu, Paris "Cuisine Diploma-Paris". https://www.cordonbleu.edu/paris/cuisine-diploma/en(2023) searched May 14, 2003.
4. "Miss Katherine Olmsted Expected Home February 25, 1927", *Sodus Record*, Volume XXX, Number 45, February 11, 1927.
5. National Archives file 2 of 2, 103.
6. Carter, 23.
7. Aberg, 480.
8. Olmsted, 18.
9. Olmsted, 19.
10.

CHAPTER 15

1. National Archives file 2 of 2, 49.
2. Olmsted, 18.
3. Le Cordon Bleu, Paris "Cuisine Diploma-Paris". https://www.cordonbleu.edu/paris/cuisine-diploma/en(2023) searched May 14, 2023.
4. *Sodus Record*, March 25, 1927.
5. Wallington, 71.
6. *Syracuse Herald American*, July 27, 1947.
7. *Sodus Record*, January 10, 1980.
8. "Interesting", *The Sodus Record*, February 1, 1918.
9. Gannett News Service, 1968.

10. *Sodus Record*, June 10, 1927.
11. Wallington, 71.
12. National Archives file 2 of 2, 66.

Continue the story with the
next book!

Miss Olmsted's Normandy Inn

Discover how Katherine Olmsted founded the Normandy Inn, from its humble beginnings through the successive ownerships over the years. The famous Normandy Inn restaurant was originally an 1800's barn, transformed into the iconic restaurant that hosted famous celebrities in the 1940s. The property has a second life today as the Sodus Feeds and Artisan's Co-op. Changes and additions are chronicled from 1927 – 2023, as well as how the business weathered major U.S. historical events; such as the Great Depression and World War II. Many interviews are included from prior owners and employees, as well as historical pictures and even French cooking recipes! This book is a treasure trove for the history buff, chef and preserver of local history.

**Pamela Lee and
husband Rich Lee**

Pamela Lee lives with her husband Richard on Tigerlily Farm and they garden avidly. A talented mathematician, Pam daylights as a banker, which helps pay the bills. She also enjoys drawing, painting, sewing and crafting. Her newfound joy is researching and writing books.

Back cover image: Katherine Olmsted's Order of the Belgian Red Cross Medal. This Belgian medal is a Patonce cross of red enamel with branches of silver oak leaves between the arms; red enamel oval, elongated vertically, in the center of the cross features a Belgian lion with superimposed white enamel shield with a red cross; suspended from a silver metal crown attached to a white ribbon with a central red stripe. 1925 Katherine Olmsted Collection, Johns Hopkins University, The Sheridan Libraries and Museums, Artifact 1006A.

www.ingramcontent.com/pod-product-compliance
Lightning Source LLC
Chambersburg PA
CBHW070517160726
48003CB00004B/1603